On My Own

PRACTICE WORKBOOK

Harcourt Brace & Company

Orlando • Atlanta • Austin • Boston • San Francisco • Chicago • Dallas • New York • Toronto • London

http://www.hbschool.com

CONTENTS

Modeling Addition or Subtraction Situations

Draw a model for each problem. Then write a number sentence to show addition or subtraction.

1. Leroy had 15 baseball cards. He gave 6 cards to Keith. How many cards does Leroy have now?

   $15 - 6 = 9$

   9 baseball cards

2. Leroy had some baseball cards. He gave 6 cards to Keith. Now Leroy has 9 cards. How many cards did he have to begin with?

   $9 + 6 = 15$

3. Leroy has 15 baseball cards. He has 9 more cards than Keith. How many cards does Keith have?

   $15 - 9 = 6$

4. Leroy has 9 more baseball cards than Keith. Keith has 6 cards. How many cards does Leroy have?

   $9 + 6 = 15$

Decide if you should add or subtract. Write the answer.

5. Joy has 14 stamps. She has 6 postcard stamps. The rest are letter stamps. How many letter stamps does she have?

   $14 - 6 = 8$ letter stamps

6. Mike had some bookmarks. He gave 4 to Jake. Now Mike has 7 bookmarks. How many bookmarks did he have to start with?

   $7 + 4 = 11$ bookmarks

7. For lunch 16 fourth graders had milk. Of these, 9 had chocolate milk. The rest had white milk. How many fourth graders had white milk for lunch?

   $16 - 9 = 7$

8. Letty had 6 pieces of tissue paper. Andy gave her 6 more pieces. How many pieces of tissue paper does Letty have in all?

   $6 + 6 = 12$ tissue paper

9. Tara had some stickers. She gave 3 to Jaspal. Now Tara has 8 stickers. How many stickers did she have to start with?

   $8 + 3 = 11$

10. Look at Problems 5 to 9. Write the number of the one that is the most like Problem 7.

    5

Using Mental Math

Vocabulary

Fill in the blank to complete the sentence.

1. An _equation_ is a number sentence that uses an equals sign to show that 2 amounts are equal.

Complete the equations. Show how you solved each one.

2. $2 + 8 = 9 + \boxed{1}$

   $10 - 9 = 1$

3. $13 - 7 = \boxed{10} - 4$

   $6 + 4 = 10$

4. $4 + \boxed{2} = 8 - 2$

   $6 - 4 = 2$

5. $11 - \boxed{4} = 12 - 5$

   $11 - 7 = 4$

6. $\boxed{9} - 3 = 2 + 4$

   $6 + 3 = 9$

7. $1 + 9 = 5 + \boxed{5}$

   $10 - 5 = 5$

Use mental math to complete each equation.

8. $3 + 4 = \boxed{5} + 2$

   $7 - 2 = 5$

9. $7 - 6 = 1 + \boxed{0}$

   $1 - 1 = 0$

10. $\boxed{4} + 4 = 6 + 2$

    $8 - 4 = 4$

11. $5 + \boxed{6} = 3 + 8$

    $11 - 5 = 6$

12. $6 + 4 = \boxed{5} + 5$

    $10 - 5 = 5$

13. $9 - \boxed{2} = 7 + 0$

    $7 +$ $9 - 9 = 2$

14. $20 - 10 = \boxed{18} - 8$

    $10 + 8 = 18$

15. $12 + 4 = 8 + \boxed{8}$

    $16 - 8 = 8$

16. $\boxed{15} - 6 = 5 + 4$

    $9 + 6 = 15$

17. $2 + 7 = 8 + \boxed{1}$

    $9 - 8 = 1$

18. $14 - 5 = 4 + \boxed{5}$

    $9 - 4 = 5$

19. $17 - \boxed{9} = 3 + 5$

    $17 - 8 = 9$

Mixed Applications

20. Brian has 7 planet stickers and 5 star stickers. Chamiko has 10 moon stickers. How many more stickers does Chamiko need to have the same number as Brian?

    2 more

21. Brian gets a package of 12 stickers. He shares them with 2 friends. Each boy gets the same number of stickers. How many does each one get?

    4 stickers

    O O O
    O O O
    O O O
    O O O
    P P P

Adding Three or More Addends

Vocabulary

Fill in the blank to complete the sentence.

1. The _Grouping promoter of Addition_ states that addends can be grouped differently but the sum does not change:

   $12 + (10 + 4) = 26$ and $(12 + 10) + 4 = 26$

Find the perimeter of each figure.

2.
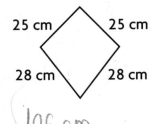
25 cm   25 cm
28 cm   28 cm

_106 cm_

3.
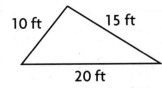
10 ft   15 ft
20 ft

_45 ft_

4.
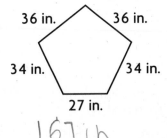
36 in.   36 in.
34 in.   34 in.
27 in.

_167 in_

5.
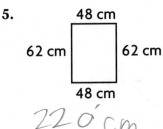
48 cm
62 cm   62 cm
48 cm

_220 cm_

6.
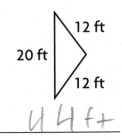
12 ft
20 ft
12 ft

_44 ft_

7.
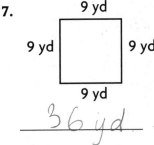
9 yd
9 yd   9 yd
9 yd

_36 yd_

Find the sum.

8. 22
    51
   +43
   ‾‾‾
    116

9. 60
    78
   +37
   ‾‾‾
    175

10. 14
     29
    +56
    ‾‾‾
     99

11. 43
     62
     43
    +62
    ‾‾‾
     120

Mixed Applications

12. Aaron runs 1 lap along the outside lines of a soccer field. What distance does Aaron run?

    _370 yd_

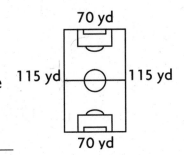
70 yd
115 yd   115 yd
70 yd

13. Yoki runs the length of the soccer field 10 times. Has she run more than or less than 1 mile? (Hint: A mile is 1,760 yd.)

    less

Problem-Solving Strategy

Make a Model

Make a model to solve.

1. Marisa is putting paper trim around a section of a bulletin board. The section is 20 inches long and 14 inches wide. How many inches of paper trim does she need?

   _____68 in._____

2. The Ling family is building a deck on their house. It will run the length of their house and have a perimeter of 108 feet. Their house is 42 feet long. How wide will the deck be?

   _____12 ft._____

3. Roy's garden has an unusual shape. The wall around it has more than 4 sides. Two of the sides are 8 feet long. The other sides are each 6 feet long. The perimeter is 40 feet. How many sides does the garden have?

   _____6 sides_____

4. Carol Sue has 86 feet of fence. She plans to use all of it to build a rectangular run for her dog. List 2 possible lengths and widths for the dog's run.

   length 30 ft. Width
   length 25 ft. width 18

Mixed Applications

Solve.

┌─────── **CHOOSE A STRATEGY** ───────┐

• **Use a Table**   • **Act It Out**   • **Make a Model**   • **Work Backward**

5. Jenny's soccer game is at one o'clock. It takes her 20 minutes to bicycle from her house to the field. If she wants to be at the field 15 minutes before the game starts, what time should she leave her house?

   12:25

6. Carl is in the second row in his class picture. He is the fourth person from the left and the fifth person from the right. How many students are in the second row?

   8 Students

Estimating Sums and Differences

Round to the nearest ten.

1. 4 ___0___ 2. 37 ___40___ 3. 55 ___60___ 4. 83 ___80___

5. 94 ___90___ 6. 79 ___80___ 7. 32 ___30___ 8. 98 ___100___

Round to the nearest hundred.

9. 88 ___100___   10. 349 _300_   11. 570 _600_

12. 725 _700_   13. 963 _1000_   14. 872 _900_

0 100 200 300 400 500 600 700 800 900 1000

Estimate the sum or difference.

15. 55 60   16. $9.99 $10.00   17. 18 20   18. 31 30
    −27 −30   − 5.00 − 5.00   +82 80   63 60
    ‾‾‾‾ 30 $5.00   ‾‾‾ 100   +96 100
                                                                   ‾‾‾‾
                                                                   1900

19. 178 200   20. 520 500   21. $21.78 $20.00   22. 978 1000
    +642 600   −209 200   + 37.03 40.00   −619 600
    ‾‾‾‾ 800   ‾‾‾‾ 300 $60.00   ‾‾‾‾ 400

23. $75.03 $80.00 24. 309 300   25. $228.75   26. $534.43
    − 35.98 40.00   472 500   + 469.26   − 372.21
            $40.00   +185 200 $200.00 $500.00
                         ‾‾‾‾ 1000   + 500.00   400.00
                                          $700.00 $700.00

Mixed Applications

27. Rylanda finds $2.39 in one pocket. She finds $6.72 in another pocket. Does she have more than or less than $10.00?

___less than___

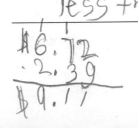

$6.72
− 2.39
$9.11

28. Rylanda has a rectangular flower garden. It has a perimeter of 32 feet. It is 6 feet wide. How long is it?

___10 ft.___

Adding and Subtracting with Money

Find the sum.

1. $6.59
   + 2.33
   $8.92

2. $8.10
   + 4.96
   $13.06

3. $14.28
   + 7.72
   $22.00

4. $11.66
   + 15.15
   $26.81

5. $3.12
   7.46
   + 3.85
   $14.43

6. $9.04
   2.25
   + 4.67
   $15.96

7. $23.97
   8.15
   + 6.39
   $38.42

8. $18.30
   19.80
   + 22.60
   $59.80

Find the difference.

9. $6.27
   − 3.42
   $2.85

10. $5.86
   − 4.39
   $1.47

11. $9.55
   − 7.89
   $1.56

12. $14.68
   − 10.90
   $3.78

13. $27.14
   − 18.33
   $8.81

14. $21.31
   − 15.74
   $5.55

15. $13.45
   − 3.50
   $9.95

16. $28.58
   − 6.70
   $1.88

Find the sum or difference.

17. $7.10
   + 3.92
   $11.02

18. $4.25
   − 3.08
   $1.17

19. $26.94
   − 10.78
   $16.16

20. $18.43
   + 7.67
   $26.00

21. $13.84
   + 24.19
   $38.03

22. $21.87
   − 9.38
   $12.48

23. $29.51
   + 21.49
   $51.00

24. $22.14
   − 14.22
   $7.92

Mixed Applications

25. Jesse's lunch cost $4.79. He received $5.21 in change. How much did he give the clerk?

$10.00

26. Jesse spent 40 minutes eating lunch. He finished at 1:10. What time did he start?

12:30

Adding and Subtracting Larger Numbers

Use addition *and* subtraction to find the missing length.

1.
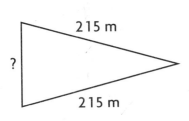
215 m
?
215 m

Perimeter = 605 m

__175__

2.
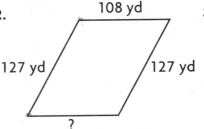
108 yd
127 yd
127 yd
?

Perimeter = 470 yd

__108__

3.
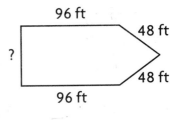
96 ft
48 ft
?
48 ft
96 ft

Perimeter = 360 ft

__72__

4.
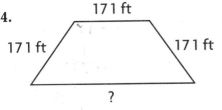
171 ft
171 ft
171 ft
?

Perimeter = 855 ft

__342__

5.
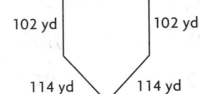
?
102 yd
102 yd
114 yd
114 yd

Perimeter = 594 yd

__162__

6.
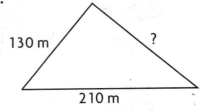
130 m
?
210 m

Perimeter = 540 m

__200__

Mixed Applications

7. The recreation center has a five-sided wading pool. Two of the pool's sides are 16 feet long and two sides are 12 feet long. The perimeter is 75 feet. What is the length of the fifth side?

__21 ft.__

8. The rectangular adult pool at the recreation center is half as wide as it is long. It is 24 feet wide. What is its perimeter?

__144 ft.__

9. The rectangular yard behind Damari's house is twice as long as it is wide. It is 48 feet wide. What is its perimeter?

__288 ft.__

10. Sara Soo has 23 pages left to read in her book. She has already read 115 pages. How many pages are in her book?

__138 pages__

115
+ 23
138

ON MY OWN P7

Subtracting Across Zeros

You may wish to use base-ten blocks to model the subtraction. Solve.

1. $\begin{array}{r} 400 \\ -381 \\ \hline 19 \end{array}$

2. $\begin{array}{r} 200 \\ -147 \\ \hline 53 \end{array}$

3. $\begin{array}{r} 500 \\ -215 \\ \hline 285 \end{array}$

4. $\begin{array}{r} 300 \\ -268 \\ \hline 32 \end{array}$

5. $\begin{array}{r} 500 \\ -373 \\ \hline 127 \end{array}$

6. $\begin{array}{r} 300 \\ -129 \\ \hline 171 \end{array}$

7. $\begin{array}{r} 400 \\ -256 \\ \hline 44 \end{array}$

8. $\begin{array}{r} 200 \\ -190 \\ \hline 10 \end{array}$

Find the difference.

9. $\begin{array}{r} 700 \\ -192 \\ \hline 508 \end{array}$

10. $\begin{array}{r} 500 \\ -246 \\ \hline 254 \end{array}$

11. $\begin{array}{r} 900 \\ -733 \\ \hline 167 \end{array}$

12. $\begin{array}{r} 600 \\ -383 \\ \hline 217 \end{array}$

13. $\begin{array}{r} 900 \\ -318 \\ \hline 582 \end{array}$

14. $\begin{array}{r} 800 \\ -710 \\ \hline 90 \end{array}$

15. $\begin{array}{r} 700 \\ -465 \\ \hline 235 \end{array}$

16. $\begin{array}{r} 600 \\ -579 \\ \hline 21 \end{array}$

17. $\begin{array}{r} 900 \\ -250 \\ \hline 50 \end{array}$

18. $\begin{array}{r} 700 \\ -382 \\ \hline 318 \end{array}$

19. $\begin{array}{r} 600 \\ -126 \\ \hline 474 \end{array}$

20. $\begin{array}{r} 800 \\ -751 \\ \hline 49 \end{array}$

Mixed Applications

21. Mr. Shea keeps a reading library in his classroom. Of the 30 books in the library, one-half are mysteries. How many of the books are not mysteries?

15 books

22. Ms. Diaz buys a box of oatmeal cookies for $2.30 and a box of molasses cookies for $2.50. She gives Laura $10.80. How much change should Laura give her?

_$6.00_

23. Laura has sold 123 boxes of cookies. If she sells 200 boxes, she will get a sweatshirt. How many more boxes of cookies does she need to sell to get a sweatshirt?

77 more

24. Lauren wants to put a border around the perimeter of her room. The room is 13 feet long and has a perimeter of 48 feet. How wide is the room?

_11 ft._

Name Emily   8/25/08

More Subtracting Across Zeros

Find the difference.

1. $\begin{array}{r} 500 \\ -166 \\ \hline 334 \end{array}$

2. $\begin{array}{r} 900 \\ -609 \\ \hline 291 \end{array}$

3. $\begin{array}{r} 200 \\ -145 \\ \hline 55 \end{array}$

4. $\begin{array}{r} 400 \\ -397 \\ \hline 03 \end{array}$

5. $\begin{array}{r} 3,000 \\ -2,780 \\ \hline 220 \end{array}$

6. $\begin{array}{r} 4,000 \\ -2,232 \\ \hline 1,768 \end{array}$

7. $\begin{array}{r} 8,000 \\ -5,004 \\ \hline 2,996 \end{array}$

8. $\begin{array}{r} 8,000 \\ -4,816 \\ \hline 1,184 \end{array}$

9. $\begin{array}{r} 5,000 \\ -1,751 \\ \hline 3,249 \end{array}$

10. $\begin{array}{r} 9,000 \\ -3,759 \\ \hline 5,241 \end{array}$

11. $\begin{array}{r} 2,000 \\ -1,265 \\ \hline 735 \end{array}$

12. $\begin{array}{r} 7,000 \\ -4,428 \\ \hline 2,572 \end{array}$

13. $\begin{array}{r} 90,000 \\ -66,536 \\ \hline 23,464 \end{array}$

14. $\begin{array}{r} 20,000 \\ -18,119 \\ \hline 1,881 \end{array}$

15. $\begin{array}{r} 30,000 \\ -10,384 \\ \hline 19,616 \end{array}$

16. $\begin{array}{r} 60,000 \\ -36,952 \\ \hline 23,048 \end{array}$

17. $\begin{array}{r} 50,000 \\ -13,747 \\ \hline 36,253 \end{array}$

18. $\begin{array}{r} 40,000 \\ -34,128 \\ \hline 5,872 \end{array}$

19. $\begin{array}{r} 10,000 \\ -8,505 \\ \hline 1,495 \end{array}$

20. $\begin{array}{r} 80,000 \\ -48,973 \\ \hline 31,027 \end{array}$

21. $\begin{array}{r} 70,004 \\ -21,274 \\ \hline 48,730 \end{array}$

22. $\begin{array}{r} 20,063 \\ -15,136 \\ \hline 4,927 \end{array}$

23. $\begin{array}{r} 60,008 \\ -19,973 \\ \hline 40,035 \end{array}$

24. $\begin{array}{r} 50,075 \\ -32,097 \\ \hline 17,978 \end{array}$

$\begin{array}{r} 20,000 \\ -1,500 \\ \hline \$18,500 \end{array}$

Mixed Applications

25. The Russell family drove their car 3,820 miles on a family trip. Before they started the trip, they had driven the car 42,151 miles. How many miles have they driven their car in all?

45,971 miles

26. The Rosner family bought a car. The list price was $20,000. The car dealership gave them a $1,500 rebate. How much did the Rosners pay for their car?

$18,500

$\begin{array}{r} 42,151 \\ +3,820 \\ \hline 45,971 \end{array}$

Problem-Solving Strategy

Work Backward

Work backward to solve.

1. Keith was 25 minutes late for band practice. He arrived at practice at 4:10 P.M. What time did band practice start?

   3:45

2. Jared ate lunch at the mall. He paid $1.29 for fruit juice, $3.59 for a tuna sandwich, and $1.75 for ice cream. He has $2.67 left. How much money did Jared have before he bought lunch?

   $9.30

3. Karen bought carnival tickets. She used 5 tickets to ride the ferris wheel, 6 tickets to go into the fun house, and 3 tickets for food. She has 11 tickets left. How many tickets did Karen begin with?

   25 tickets

4. Curtis and Ellie made some flyers for their yard sale. Curtis put up 12 flyers around the neighborhood and Ellie put up 19 flyers. They had 9 flyers left. How many flyers did they make?

   40 flyers

Mixed Applications

Solve.

CHOOSE A STRATEGY
• Draw a Picture • Act It Out • Make a Model • Work Backward

5. The school bus stops at the corner of Ashley's street between 7:40 and 7:55 each morning. It takes Ashley 5 minutes to walk to the bus stop. What is the latest time she can leave her house if she wants to be sure of catching the bus?

   7:35

6. Renee is making brownies. It takes 10 minutes to mix the ingredients and 35 minutes to bake the brownies. She then lets them cool for a half hour. What time should Renee start making the brownies if she wants to be finished at 3:30 P.M.?

   2:15

Estimating Sums and Differences

Round to the nearest *hundred*.

1. 379
 400

2. 862
 900

3. 529
 500

4. 613
 600

Round to the nearest *thousand*.

5. 3,030
 3000

6. 5,919
 6000

7. 9,476
 9000

8. 4,489
 4000

Estimate the sum or difference.

9. 379 400
  − 150 −200
    200

10. 721 700
  + 496 +500
    1200

11. 1,811 2,000
  + 6,503 1,000
    9,000

12. 5,625 6,000
  − 2,175 −2,000
    4,000

13. 6,438 6,000
  − 5,382 −5,000
    1,000

14. 936 900
  − 779 −800
    100

15. 160 200
   811   800
  + 306 +300
    1300

16. 2,516 3,000
   2,790 3,000
  + 2,345 2,000
    8,000

17. 8,448 8,000
  − 4,796 −5,000
    3,000

Mixed Applications

18. On Thursday Emil earned $6.50 dog-walking. On Saturday he earned $15.75 raking. That brought his earnings for the week to $34.50. How much had he earned before Thursday?

    $12.25

19. Jessica has saved $114. She needs to save $225 to pay her share of the cost for soccer camp. Estimate to find about how much more she has to save.

    $100

20. If there are 1,000 miles between Princeton and Foxboro, how many miles are between Princeton and Ladd?

    600 miles

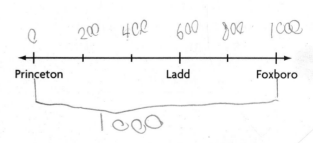

0   200   400   600   800   1000

Princeton   Ladd   Foxboro

1000

ON MY OWN

Choosing the Operation

Write if you should *add* or *subtract* the missing numbers to solve.
Then use the information in the table to find the missing numbers
and solve the problems.

1. J. Houlihan scored _?_ career
   points. C. Ashmead scored _?_
   career points. <u>How many more
   points did Houlihan score than
   Ashmead?</u>

   370 more

2. S. Lewis scored _?_ career
   (2,253)
   points. Together, M. Wisentaner
   and K. Diaz scored _?_ career
   (2,418)
   points. Did Lewis score more
   points than Wisentaner and
   Diaz combined?

   _NO_

Basketball Player	Points Scored During College Career
S. Lewis	2,253
J. Houlihan	1,909
N. Razelan	1,578
C. Ashmead	1,539
A. Boenitz	1,354
M. Wisentaner	1,217
K. Diaz	1,201

Use the information in the table to find the missing numbers and
solve the problem.

Sports Complex	Capacity
Lexington Arena	23,600
Appleton Center	28,400
Springs Centrum	32,100
Mendez Stadium	35,700

4. The difference in the capacities
   of the Mendez Stadium and the
   Springs Centrum is _?_. The
   difference in capacity between
   the Appleton Center and the
   Lexington Arena is _?_. Which
   two sports complexes have the
   greatest difference in capacity?

   Lexington Arena

   Appeton Center

3. The capacity of the Lexington
   Arena is _?_. The capacity of
   the Appleton Center is _?_. Is
   the capacity of these two sport
   complexes together greater than
   or less than 50,000 people?

   greater than

Name _____

What Questions Can Multiplication Answer?

Model each problem. Solve.

1. Mr. Chou drives 5 miles in all to work and back each day. How many miles does he drive to work and back in 5 days?

25 days

2. Bill is making 6 salads. He puts 3 olives in each salad. How many olives will he use in all?

8 olives

3. Ivan brushes his cat 3 times each week. In 4 weeks, how many times does he brush his cat?

12 times

4. Rosa is making 8 bracelets. She uses 2 green beads for each bracelet. How many green beads does she need?

16 more

5. Larry bought 2 packs of hockey cards. Each pack has 6 cards in it. How many cards did Larry buy in all?

12 cards

6. Linda has 2 basketball shirts and 4 pairs of shorts. How many different outfits can she wear to play basketball?

2 shirts

Mixed Applications

7. Ryan is fourth in line for the water fountain. There are 6 people in the line. How many people are in line in front of Ryan?

3 people

8. Liz and her dog together weigh 92 pounds. Liz weighs 73 pounds. How much does her dog weigh?

21 pounds

9. The price of a movie ticket for an adult is $7.50. The price of a child's ticket is $3.75. Beth is going to the movies with her mother. How much will they pay for tickets?

$11.25

10. A rectangular wall surrounds a garden. The length of the wall is 62 feet, and the width is 44 feet. What is the perimeter of the garden?

212 ft.

Multiplication Properties

Vocabulary

Write *a*, *b*, or *c* to tell which property is shown.

   a. Property of One   **b. Zero Property**   **c. Order Property**

1. $8 \times 3 = 3 \times 8$ __C__   2. $1 \times 360 = 360$ __a__   3. $0 \times 76 = 0$ __b__

Use the multiplication properties to solve.

4. $\begin{array}{r} 9 \\ \times\ 1 \\ \hline 9 \end{array}$ 5. $\begin{array}{r} 1 \\ \times\ 5 \\ \hline 5 \end{array}$ 6. $\begin{array}{r} 0 \\ \times\ 8 \\ \hline 0 \end{array}$ 7. $\begin{array}{r} 3 \\ \times\ 0 \\ \hline 0 \end{array}$

8. $\begin{array}{r} 4 \\ \times\ 1 \\ \hline 4 \end{array}$ 9. $\begin{array}{r} 0 \\ \times\ 7 \\ \hline 0 \end{array}$ 10. $\begin{array}{r} 2 \\ \times\ 1 \\ \hline 2 \end{array}$ 11. $\begin{array}{r} 12 \\ \times\ 0 \\ \hline 0 \end{array}$

12. $5 \times 6 =$ __30__   13. $2 \times 8 =$ __16__   14. $4 \times 7 =$ __28__   15. $9 \times 3 =$ __27__

   $6 \times 5 =$ __30__ $8 \times 2 =$ __16__ $7 \times 4 =$ __28__ $3 \times 9 =$ __27__

Mixed Applications

16. Kara used 4 each of 5 different-colored beads for a necklace. Lucy used 5 each of 4 different-colored beads for her necklace. How many more beads did Kara use than Lucy?

   __Same__

17. Anthony decorated his belt with 5 rows of beads. Each row had 6 beads in it. There were 2 rows of blue beads, 2 rows of red beads, and 1 row of white beads. How many white beads did Anthony use?

   __6 white beads__

18. Li spent $15.95 for a model plane kit and $17.59 for a model car kit. He had $1.46 left. How much money did Li have before he bought the kits?

   __$35.00__

19. Sandy bought some clay for $9.99 and a jar of glaze for $6.49. She gave the clerk $20.00. How much change will she get?

   __$3.52__

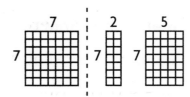

More About Multiplication Models

Use the arrays. Find the products.

1. $7 \times 8 =$ ___?___

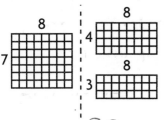

$4 \times 8 =$ _32_

$3 \times 8 =$ _24_

So, $7 \times 8 =$ _5 6_.

2. $7 \times 7 =$ ___?___

$7 \times 2 =$ _14_

$7 \times 5 =$ _35_

So, $7 \times 7 =$ _4 9_.

Use grid paper. Break apart the numbers to find the product.

3. $7 \times 6 =$ _42_ $2 \times 6 = 12$ $5 \times 6 = 30$

4. $8 \times 9 =$ _72_

5. $5 \times 8 =$ _40_

6. $8 \times 8 =$ _64_ $3 \times 8 = 24 + 5 \times 8 = 40$

7. $5 \times 9 =$ _45_

8. $8 \times 6 =$ _48_ $5 \times 8 = 40$ $1 \times 8 = 8$

9. $6 \times 9 =$ _54_

10. $7 \times 9 =$ _63_

Mixed Applications

11. Trudy had 19 nickels. She loaned 50¢ to her sister. How much money does Trudy have now?

_45¢_

12. Christy walks 8 laps around the track. It takes her 7 minutes to walk each lap. How much time in all does Christy walk?

56 min.

Multiplying Three Factors

Vocabulary

Complete.

1. When the grouping of factors is changed, the product
   remains the same. This is called the _grouping pRoperty_.

Find the product.

2. $(3 \times 2) \times 3 =$ _18_

3. $(3 \times 1) \times 7 =$ _21_

4. $(4 \times 2) \times 2 =$ _16_

Show two ways to group Exercises 5–7 using parentheses ( ).
Find the products.

5. $9 \times 2 \times 1 =$ _?_

   $(9 \times 2) \times 1 = 18$

   $9 \times (2 \times 1) = 18$

6. $6 \times 5 \times 1 =$ _?_

   $(6 \times 5) \times 1 = 30$

   $6 \times (5 \times 1) = 30$

7. $3 \times 4 \times 2 =$ _?_

   $(3 \times 4) \times 2 = 24$

   $3 \times (4 \times 2) = 24$

Use the Grouping Property to solve each problem.

8. $(5 \times 4) \times 1 =$ _?_

   $(5 \times 4) \times 1 = 20$

   $5 \times (4 \times 1) = 20$

9. $(3 \times 8) \times 1 =$ _?_

   $(3 \times 8) \times 1 = 24$

   $3 \times (8 \times 1) = 24$

10. $2 \times (3 \times 3) =$ _?_

    $(2 \times 3) \times 3 = 18$

    $2 \times (3 \times 3) = 18$

Mixed Applications

11. The students in Ms. Li's class
    filled out a pet survey. They
    found that 1 student had 3 pets,
    4 students had 2 pets, and 9
    students had 1 pet. How many
    students had pets?

    14 Students

12. The fourth-grade classroom in
    the Payson Park School has
    6 rows of desks. Each row has
    5 desks. How many desks are
    there in all?

    30 desks

Problem-Solving Strategy

Make a Model

Make a model to solve.

1. On Pine Street 4 children are decorating their bikes for a parade. Each bike has 2 wheels. The children will tape 4 pieces of ribbon to the spokes of each wheel. How many pieces of ribbon will they need?

   32 pieces of ribbon

2. Lisa feeds her dog 2 times a day. It takes her 3 minutes to prepare the food each time. How many minutes does Lisa spend feeding her dog each week?

   42 min.

3. At the start of a garage sale there were 2 boxes of magazines. In each box were 2 stacks of magazines. There were 7 magazines in each stack. How many magazines were there at the start of the garage sale?

   28 magazines

4. In Jeff's backyard there are 2 trees. On each tree is 1 bird feeder. It takes 7 handfuls of seeds to fill each bird feeder. How many handfuls of seed does Jeff need to fill the bird feeders?

   14 handfuls

Mixed Applications

Solve.

┌─── **CHOOSE A STRATEGY** ───┐

• **Find a Pattern**   • **Work Backward**   • **Draw a Picture**   • **Write a Number Sentence**   • **Make a Model**

5. Donna is stringing beads to make a bracelet. She strings 3 red beads followed by 2 yellow beads. She plans to use 20 beads in all for her bracelet. How many beads will be red?

   12 red beads

6. The Plymouth Panthers made 15 points in the second quarter of the basketball game. They made 22 points in the third quarter, and 19 points in the fourth quarter. They made 72 points in all during the game. How many points did they make in the first quarter?

   16 points

Name _____

Choosing the Operation

Choose the number sentence you would use to solve Problems 1–4. Then solve.

a. $7 \times 5 = \underline{}$ b. $7 - \underline{} = 5$ c. $7 + 5 = \underline{}$ d. $7 - 5 = \underline{}$

1. The Red Sox made 7 runs in the baseball game. The White Sox made fewer runs than the Red Sox. The Red Sox won by 5 runs. How many runs did the White Sox make?

   B 2

2. The Seals made 7 runs in the last inning. Before the last inning, they had made 5 runs. What was the Seals' score at the end of the game?

   c 12

3. The Hawks have 7 away games this month and 5 home games. How many more away games than home games do they have?

   d 2

4. Behind home plate there are 5 rows of seats. Each row has 7 seats in it. How many seats are in this section?

   A 35

Mixed Applications

5. Mike paid $9 for a baseball cap. Meg paid $6 for one. How much more did Mike pay than Meg?

   $3 more

6. Lex had 2 quarters, 3 dimes, 1 nickel, and 4 pennies. Did he have more than or less than $1?

   less than

7. In the pottery classroom there were 3 tables. There were 6 people sitting at each table. Each person made 2 clay animals. How many clay animals did they make in all?

   36 animals

8. Mr. Magri drove 6 miles to the gas station. Then he drove 4 miles to the library. He left the library and drove 9 miles to his home. How many miles did Mr. Magri drive in all?

   19 mil.

9. The perimeter of Eric's room is 46 feet. The length of his room is 15 feet. Will a rug that is 12 feet by 10 feet fit in his room?

   No

10. The video is 105 minutes long. Jacki has watched 40 minutes of it. How many more minutes are left on the video?

    65 more min.

What Questions Can Division Answer?

Decide whether using division will answer the question. Write *yes* or *no*. If you write *yes*, then solve.

1. Inez is going to ride her bike 45 miles. She plans to stop to take a drink of water every 5 miles. How many times will she stop for water?

   yes   9 times

2. There are 14 children playing tennis. Each child plays with a partner. How many partner pairs are there?

   yes   7 pairs

3. Nicole bought 2 packages of thank-you cards. One package had 8 cards in it. The other package had 12 cards in it. How many thank-you cards did Nicole buy?

   No   20 cards

4. Connor is decorating 6 cupcakes with jelly beans. He has 24 jelly beans. He wants to put the same quantity on each cupcake. How many jelly beans should he put on each?

   yes   4 jelly beans

5. Luke has 35 pennies. He's sorting them into groups of 5 to trade them for nickels. How many groups can he make?

   yes   7 groups

6. The floor of Alice's treehouse has a perimeter of 36 feet. Its shape is a square. What is the length of each side?

   yes   9 ft.

Mixed Applications

7. A single-scoop ice-cream cone costs $1.79. A double-scoop ice cream cone costs $2.15. How much more does the double-scoop cost than the single-scoop?

   _36¢_

8. Ray lives 20 minutes from the post office. On Friday, he walked to the post office and back. He spent 5 minutes inside the post office. When he got home, it was 4:30. At what time did he leave for the post office?

   _3:45_

Name _____ inverse _____

Connecting Multiplication and Division

Vocabulary

Complete each sentence.

1. Division undoes multiplication. Division is the
   _____ invers _____ of multiplication.

2. A set of related multiplication and division sentences
   using the same numbers is a _____ fact family _____

Write a related multiplication fact.

3. $21 \div 3 = 7$
$7 \times 3 = 21$

4. $25 \div 5 = 5$
$5 \times 5 = 25$

5. $16 \div 8 = 2$
$8 \times 2 = 16$

6. $18 \div 6 = 3$
$6 \times 3 = 18$

7. $54 \div 9 = 6$
$9 \times 6 = 54$

8. $16 \div 4 = 4$
$4 \times 4 = 16$

9. $12 \div 2 = 6$
$2 \times 6 = 12$

10. $35 \div 7 = 5$
$5 \times 7 = 35$

Complete the number sentence. Write the multiplication fact used
to find the quotient.

11. $8 \div 4 = 2$
$4 \times 2 = 8$

12. $24 \div 6 = 4$
$6 \times 4 = 24$

13. $30 \div 5 = 6$
$6 \times 5 = 30$

14. $48 \div 8 = 6$
$8 \times 6 = 48$

Write the fact family for each set of numbers.

15. 3, 4, 12
$3 \times 4 = 12$ $12 \div 4 = 3$
$4 \times 3 = 12$ $12 \div 3 = 4$

16. 4, 7, 28
$4 \times 7 = 28$ $28 \div 7 = 4$
$7 \times 4 = 28$ $28 \div 4 = 7$

Mixed Applications

17. Four laps around the track is a
    mile. Norice ran 12 laps. How
    many miles did she run?

    _____ 43 miles _____

18. Tucker has 4 shirts and 2 vests.
    How many different shirt-vest
    combinations can he wear?

    _____ 8 combinations _____

Dividing with Remainders

Vocabulary

Circle the word that is incorrect in the following sentence. Write the correct word.

1. The amount left over when you find the quotient is called the dividend. _remainder_

Use counters to find the quotient and remainder.

2. $13 \div 4 =$ _3 r 1_   3. $19 \div 4 =$ _4 r 3_   4. $26 \div 6 =$ _4 r 2_

5. $14 \div 3 =$ _4 r 2_   6. $30 \div 9 =$ _3 r 3_   7. $31 \div 5 =$ _6 r 1_

Use the model to find the quotient.

8. $13 \div 5 =$ _2 r 3_   9. $15 \div 2 =$ _7 r 1_

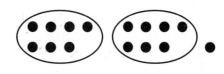

Find the quotient. You may wish to use a model to help you.

10. $18 \div 5 =$ _3 r 3_   11. $17 \div 4 =$ _4 r 1_   12. $25 \div 8 =$ _3 r 1_

13. $17 \div 6 =$ _2 r 4_   14. $11 \div 2 =$ _5 r 1_   15. $14 \div 6 =$ _2 r 2_

16. $23 \div 5 =$ _4 r 3_   17. $22 \div 3 =$ _7 r 1_   18. $29 \div 4 =$ _7 r 1_

Mixed Applications

19. Elliot and Kenji are each making a mask. Elliot plans to put 5 feathers on his mask. Kenji plans to put 8 feathers on his mask. How many feathers will they need in all?

    13 feathers

20. Trudy, Lise, and Axel need to make 17 pumpkins to use as decorations. They each made 5 pumpkins. How many do they still need?

    2 more

Problem-Solving Strategy

Make a Table

Make a table to solve.

1. Together, Lena and Alexis are saving money to buy a CD player that costs $96. Lena saves $5 each week. Alexis saves $3 each week. How many weeks will it take them to save enough money?

   12 weeks

2. A subway train leaves the station every 20 minutes starting at 3 P.M. Beverly arrives at the station at 5:15 P.M. At what time does the first train she will be able to get on leave the station?

   5:20

3. Cameron bought a granola bar for $0.49. How many different ways can he pay for it using only dimes, nickels, and pennies? He will give the clerk the exact amount, at least one of each coin, and no more than 9 pennies.

   7 ways

4. Keith is placing 20 books on a bookcase. He will use either 3, 4, or 5 shelves in the case. How many ways can he arrange the books so the same number of books are on each shelf? Describe each way.

   4 shelves with 5 books each
   5 shelves with 4 books each

Mixed Applications

Solve.

CHOOSE A STRATEGY

- Find a Pattern
- Make a Table
- Make a Model
- Write a Number Sentence

5. Jason is making a price list for audiotapes. He plans to sell 1 tape for $2.00, 2 tapes for $3.80, and 3 tapes for $5.60. If he continues pricing this way, at what price will he sell 5 tapes?

   $9.20

6. There are 2 windows at the entrance to the video store. Each window has 3 sections. The owner will put up 2 posters in each section. How many posters will she put up?

   12 posters

Division on a Multiplication Table

Find the quotient. You may wish to use the multiplication table to help you.

Multiplication Table

×	0	1	2	3	4	5	6	7	8	9
0	0	0	0	0	0	0	0	0	0	0
1	0	1	2	3	4	5	6	7	8	9
2	0	2	4	6	8	10	12	14	16	18
3	0	3	6	9	12	15	18	21	24	27
4	0	4	8	12	16	20	24	28	32	36
5	0	5	10	15	20	25	30	35	40	45
6	0	6	12	18	24	30	36	42	48	54
7	0	7	14	21	28	35	42	49	56	63
8	0	8	16	24	32	40	48	56	64	72
9	0	9	18	27	36	45	54	63	72	81

1. $30 \div 5 = \underline{6}$

2. $28 \div 7 = \underline{4}$

3. $42 \div 6 = \underline{7}$

4. $21 \div 3 = \underline{7}$

5. $72 \div 8 = \underline{9}$

6. $54 \div 6 = \underline{9}$ 7. $40 \div 5 = \underline{8}$ 8. $24 \div 8 = \underline{3}$ 9. $49 \div 7 = \underline{7}$

10. $27 \div 9 = \underline{3}$ 11. $36 \div 4 = \underline{9}$ 12. $36 \div 6 = \underline{6}$ 13. $28 \div 7 = \underline{4}$

14. $42 \div 7 = \underline{6}$ 15. $48 \div 8 = \underline{6}$ 16. $20 \div 5 = \underline{4}$ 17. $40 \div 8 = \underline{5}$

18. $35 \div 7 = \underline{5}$ 19. $45 \div 9 = \underline{5}$ 20. $24 \div 4 = \underline{6}$ 21. $32 \div 8 = \underline{4}$

Mixed Applications

22. There are 24 desks in Mr. Brett's classroom. He wants to arrange them so there are more than 2 rows, but fewer than 10 rows. Each row will have the same number of desks. In how many different ways can he do this?

    3, 4, 6, or 8 rows

23. The Drama Club held a car wash to raise money. The club members charged $4 per car. Between 10:00 A.M. and 11:00 A.M. they earned $28. How many cars did they wash?

    7 cars

24. Abigail bought 5 packages of videotapes. Each package had 3 tapes. Clarence bought 2 packages of videotapes. Each package had 6 tapes in it. Who bought more videotapes?

    Abigail

25. At the music store, Bruce looked at CDs. He spent 10 minutes in the classical section and 15 minutes in the jazz section. He left the store at 3:10. What time did he arrive at the music store?

    2:45

Recording and Practicing Division

Find the quotient.

1. $36 \div 9 = \underline{4}$ 2. $4 \div 1 = \underline{4}$ 3. $42 \div 7 = \underline{6}$ 4. $5 \div 5 = \underline{1}$

5. $18 \div 6 = \underline{3}$ 6. $8 \div 8 = \underline{1}$ 7. $45 \div 9 = \underline{5}$ 8. $24 \div 4 = \underline{6}$

9. $40 \div 5 = \underline{8}$ 10. $56 \div 8 = \underline{7}$ 11. $64 \div 8 = \underline{8}$ 12. $21 \div 7 = \underline{3}$

13. $36 \div 6 = \underline{6}$ 14. $72 \div 9 = \underline{8}$ 15. $9 \div 1 = \underline{9}$ 16. $48 \div 8 = \underline{6}$

17. $27 \div 3 = \underline{9}$ 18. $28 \div 4 = \underline{7}$ 19. $30 \div 6 = \underline{5}$ 20. $24 \div 3 = \underline{8}$

21. $7\overline{)7}$ 22. $9\overline{)63}$ 23. $1\overline{)6}$ 24. $7\overline{)49}$ 25. $2\overline{)16}$

26. $5\overline{)45}$ 27. $3\overline{)3}$ 28. $8\overline{)32}$ 29. $6\overline{)54}$ 30. $8\overline{)72}$

31. $4\overline{)32}$ 32. $1\overline{)5}$ 33. $7\overline{)56}$ 34. $5\overline{)35}$ 35. $9\overline{)54}$

Mixed Applications

36. Tomatoes were $1 for each pound. Mrs. Mendez paid $6 for tomatoes. How many pounds did she buy?

6 pound

37. Ray had $5 to spend on food and drinks at the movies. He bought popcorn for $2.75 and 2 drinks for $0.99 each. How much money did he have left?

27¢

38. Fredda and Sylvia are setting up chairs for a concert. They are placing 8 chairs in each row. There are 72 chairs. How many rows can they make?

9 rows

39. Ashley sold 14 tickets to the play. Christine sold 12 tickets, and Laurel sold 13 tickets. How many tickets did the 3 girls sell in all?

39 tickets

40. Paul's dog, Bowser, was 8 years old in 1997. When was Bowser born?

1989

41. Melanie practices the flute 4 hours each week. Jennifer practices the flute 3 hours each week. How much longer does Melanie practice in 4 weeks than Jennifer does?

4 hours more

Choosing the Operation

Choose an operation to use. Then solve.

1. The fine for an overdue book at the Cotter Library is 5¢ a day. Tyler returned his books 1 day late. He paid a 30¢ fine. How many books did he return?

   6 books

2. Clyde sleeps 8 hours each night. How many hours does he sleep each week?

   56 hours

3. Kate sold 21 boxes of cookies. Randy sold 32 boxes of cookies. Gina sold 49 boxes of cookies. How many boxes did they sell in all?

   102 boxes

4. On Tuesday morning, Mrs. Corbett drove 57 miles to Princeton. In the afternoon she drove to Natick. She drove a total of 90 miles. How many miles was it from Princeton to Natick?

   33 miles

Mixed Applications

5. Winona has 4 different colors of papers and 3 different colors of envelopes. How many different paper-envelope combinations can she make?

   12 combinations

6. Peter took a three-day 28-mile backpacking trip. He hiked 9 miles the first day and 11 miles the second day. How many miles did he hike the third day?

   8 miles

7. Jason and Chuck are playing a game. They have each taken four turns. Jason has scored 8 points, 8 points, 3 points, and 5 points. Chuck has scored 7 points, 4 points, 9 points, and 5 points. Which player has scored more points?

   Chuck

8. Ms. Trent's class is divided into 6 teams for the math fair. Each team has 3 jobs to complete to get ready for the fair. How many jobs in all do the teams have to complete?

   18 jobs

How Numbers Are Used

Tell whether each number is *cardinal*, *ordinal*, or *nominal*.

1. channel 56

nominal

2. 31 Oak St.

nominal

3. $50

cardinal

4. 6th row

ordinal

Write the weight, length, or temperature shown.

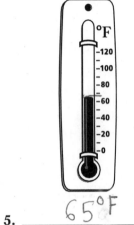

5. _____ 65°F

6. _____ 2 ft.

7. _____ 3 lbs

8. _____ 10°C

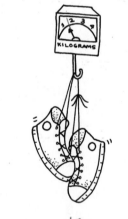

9. _____ 1.5 Kg

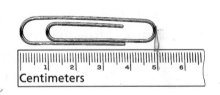

10. _____ 5 cm.

Mixed Applications

11. Fall begins in the ninth month of the year and ends in the twelfth month. Name the months in which fall begins and ends.

Sept. Dec.

12. Cindy delivers newspapers to 6 houses on each of 4 streets. How many newspapers does she deliver?

24 newspapers

Name _____

More About How Numbers Are Used

Vocabulary

Complete the sentence.

1. The location of a point on a grid can be found using two numbers called an __ordered pair__.

The key below shows who lives at each house.

A = Avery   G = Guy

B = Bonnie   H = Ho

C = Carlos   I = Inez

D = Delle   J = Jerry

E = Ethan   K = Kyle

F = Felix   L = Lynn

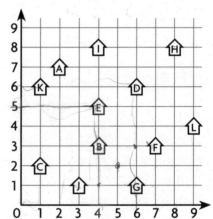

Use the map to write the ordered pair for the location of each person's house.

2. Ethan (4, 5)

3. Inez (4, 8)

4. Delle (6, 6)

5. Avery (2, 7)

6. Carlos (1, 2)

7. Lynn (9, 4)

Write the name of the person who lives at the location of the ordered pair.

8. (7, 3) Felix

9. (4, 3) Bonnie

10. (8, 8) Ho

11. (3, 1) Jerry

12. (1, 6) Kyle

13. (6, 1) Guy

Mixed Applications

14. What are three possible locations for Miko's house? Her house is an equal distance from Bonnie's house and from Guy's house.

(4, 1) (5, 2) (6, 3)

15. In the dining hall there were 2 rows of tables. There were 4 tables in each row. On each table was a vase with 3 roses. How many roses were there in all?

24 roses

Understanding 1,000

Look in your "1,000 Squares" book. Write the page number on which each number is found.

1. 4 ___1___ 2. 40 ___1___ 3. 400 ___4___

4. 726 ___8___ 5. 333 ___4___ 6. 983 ___1,000___

7. 499 ___5___ 8. 500 ___5___ 9. 501 ___6___

10. 110 ___2___ 11. 210 ___3___ 12. 310 ___4___

Mixed Applications

For Problems 13–18, use your "1,000 Squares" book.

13. Ms. Tang's class is collecting aluminum cans for recycling. They have collected 348 cans. On what page in your book is 348?

___page 4___

14. The goal of Ms. Tang's class is to collect 500 cans in all. How many more cans do they need to collect if they now have 348 cans? On what page in your book is that number?

___page 2 – 152___

15. Miss Betts' class has collected 476 pounds of newspapers for the recycling program. Mr. Craig's class has collected 337 pounds of newspapers. On what page of your book is the number of pounds the two classes have collected together?

___page 9___

16. The first month Mrs. Alvarado's class collected newspapers, they collected 50 pounds. The second month they collected 110 pounds, and the third month they collected 170 pounds. If the pattern continues, how many pounds will they collect the fourth month?

___230___

17. How many more pounds of newspapers has Miss Betts' class collected than Mr. Craig's class? On what page of your book is that number?

___139 – page 2___

18. For every can Ms. Tang's class recycles, they receive a nickel. How many cans do they need to recycle to receive $1? $10? $100?

___20 cans, 200 cans, 2000 can___

More About 1,000

Write the number shown by the base-ten blocks.

1.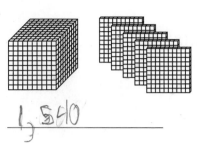

1,540

2.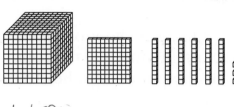

1,163

Record the number of thousands, hundreds, tens, and ones.

3. 4,728

4,000

700

20

8

4. 7,097

7,000

0

90

7

5. 1,661

1,000

600

60

1

Put in the comma, and write each number in words.

6. 2,5 3 2   two thousand, five hundred thirty - two

7. 8,6 1 0   eight thousand, six hundred ten

8. 6,1 7 5   six thousand, one hundred seventy - five

9. 3,4 0 4   three thousand, four hundred - four

Mixed Applications

10. In the summer Rocky Port has a population of about 4,600 people. In the winter the population is about 2,800 people. About how many more people live in Rocky Port in the summer than in the winter?

1,800 people

11. Write the number that is 2,000 less than seven thousand, two hundred fifty-six.

5,256

Problem-Solving Strategy

Act It Out

Act it out to solve.

1. Patricia takes a sheet of paper and folds it in half, folds it in half again, and folds it in half a third time. When she unfolds the paper, into how many sections will the sheet

   be divided? _____8_____

2. Eduardo and Tim are playing a counting game. They are counting to 30. Eduardo claps when they say a number that can be divided by 3. Tim claps when they say a number that can be divided by 4. On what numbers do

   they both clap? __12, 24__

3. Bijal is going from her home to the computer store. To get to the store, she walks 3 blocks west and 2 blocks south. When she leaves the store, she walks 3 blocks east. How many blocks and in what direction should she

   walk to get home? __2 blocks N__

Mixed Applications

Solve.

CHOOSE A STRATEGY

- Make a Model   • Write a Number Sentence   • Act It Out   • Find a Pattern

4. The distance from Chicago to New York City is 820 miles. The distance from Chicago to Phoenix, Arizona, is 1,800 miles. Is the difference in distances greater than or less than 1,000 miles?

   __Less then__

5. The perimeter of Ms. Wong's rectangular vegetable garden is 76 feet. What could be the length and width of her garden? List two possible answers.

   __30 x 8__

   __25 x 13__

Name Emily   10/1/08

Benchmark Numbers

Vocabulary

Fill in the blank.

1. A benchmark number is a point of reference.
   Benchmark numbers are often used to show number
   relationships.

Write a benchmark number for each problem. Use the benchmark
to estimate.

A [image diagram]

B [image diagram]

C [image diagram]

2. In which train are there about
   20 connecting cubes?

   B

3. About how many cubes are in
   train C?

   about 40

Write *more than* or *less than* for each.

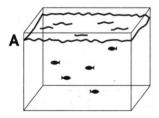
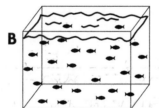
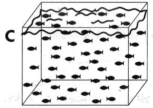

4. Are there more than or less
   than 15 fish in tank B?

   more than

5. Are there more than or less
   than 75 fish in tank C?

   less than

Mixed Applications

6. There are 21 kernels of popcorn
   in Darla's hand. If she takes about
   the same amount each time, how
   many handfuls will it take to get
   about 100 kernels?

   5

7. Chet is making 8 salads. He cut
   40 tomato wedges. How many
   tomato wedges will he put in
   each salad if he puts the same
   number of wedges in each?

   5 tw.

Numeration Systems

Vocabulary

Fill in the blank to complete the sentence.

1. A _Numeration system_
   is a way of naming numbers and counting.

Egyptian	𓏲	◡	∧		
Standard	1,000	100	10	1

Write the value of each group of Egyptian symbols.

2. ||| _____3_____

3. ∧∧||| _____23_____

4. ◡◡| _____201_____

5. 𓏲𓏲∧∧∧|| _____2,032_____

6. 𓏲𓏲𓏲◡|| _____3,102_____

7. 𓏲||||| _____1,005_____

Show the value of each digit in a place-value system.

8. 307

$7 \times 1 = 7$

$0 \times 10 = 0$

$3 \times 100 = 300$

9. 15

$5 \times 1 = 5$

$1 \times 10 = 10$

10. 356

$6 \times 1 = 6$

$5 \times 10 = 50$

$3 \times 100 = 300$

11. 1,205

$5 \times 1 = 5$

$0 \times 10 = 0$

$2 \times 100 = 200$

$1 \times 1,000 = 1,000$

Mixed Applications

12. The Pyramid of Khufu is 450 feet high. The Statue of Liberty is 302 feet high. How much higher is the pyramid? Write the answer, using both numeration systems.

    _148, ◡∧∧∧||||||||_

13. John built a model of a pyramid with a square bottom. The length of each side of the bottom is 8 inches. What is the distance around the bottom of the pyramid?

    32 inches

Name _Emily_   _10/17/08_

Reading and Writing Numbers

Vocabulary

Write the correct letter from Column 2 that describes each number.

Column 1		**Column 2**
1. 439	_C_	**a.** expanded form
2. 400 + 30 + 9	_A_	**b.** written form
3. four hundred thirty-nine	_b_	**c.** standard form

Write each number in standard form.

4. fifty-six _56_   5. five hundred thirty-three _533_

6. thirty-seven _37_   7. six thousand, two hundred eighty-one _6,281_

8. two hundred three _203_   9. five thousand, fifty-six _5,056_

Write each number in expanded form.

10. 37 _30+7_   11. 627 _600+20+7_

12. 4,209 _4,000+200+9_   13. 6,056 _6,000+50+6_

Write each number in two other ways.

14. five hundred sixty-one

_561_

_500+60+1_

15. 5,607

five thousand, six hundred seven

_5000+600+7_

Mixed Applications

16. Anne paid $19 each for two guinea pigs and $69 for a cage. Write in standard form and in written form the total amount she spent.

$107— one hundred seven dollars

17. The distance around a rectangular field is 2,000 feet. The length is 800 feet. What is the width?

_200 ft._

Mental Math and Place Value

Use place value to name each number in two different ways.

1. 150

1 hundred 5 tens

15 tens

2. 560

5 hundreds 6 tens

56 tens

3. 2,100

21 hundreds

210 tens

4. 3,600

36 hundreds

360 tens

5. 180

1 hundred 8 tens

18 tens

6. 2,900

29 hundreds

290 tens

Use another name for each number and solve by using mental math.

7. 300
+800

$\boxed{3}$ hundreds
8 hundreds
11 hundreds

8. 900
+600

9 hundreds
6 hundreds
15 hundreds

9. 6,000
+3,000

6 thousands
3 thousands
9 thousands

10. 4,100
+2,300

$\boxed{41}$ hundreds
23 hundreds
64 hundreds

Mixed Applications

11. A fourth-grade class collected 4,500 pennies to buy new library books. How many dollars do the pennies equal?

_$45_

12. John sold lemonade for 10 cents a cup. He sold 50 cups of lemonade. How much money did he earn?

_$5_

Place Value to 100,000

Write *true* or *false* for each statement. Rewrite false statements to make them true.

1. There are exactly 10 ~~ten~~ *one* thousands in 10,000.

   false
   _____

   _____

2. There are exactly 100 thousands in 100,000.

   true
   _____

   _____

Mixed Applications

3. Each shelf in a library holds about 100 books. About how many shelves are needed to hold 10,000 books?

   100

4. It takes John about 10 minutes to read each chapter in a book. About how many chapters can John read in an hour?

   6 chapters

5. On Monday Anne borrowed 12 books from the library. On Friday she returned 9 books and borrowed 5 more. How many library books does she have now?

   8 . books

6. A square farm is 100,000 cm on each side. How long is a fence that goes all the way around the farm?

   400,000 cm

7. Carrie wants to buy paint. Two of the paint tubes cost $3.95 each, and the other tube costs $2.25. Carrie has ten dollars. Does she have enough money to buy all three tubes of paint?

   No

8. Two classes read books for a month. One class read 120 books, the other class read 150 books. How many books did the two classes read in all?

   270 books

Using Large Numbers

Vocabulary

Fill in the blank to complete the sentence.

1. A _period_ is a group of three numbers in a large number.

Write the number as you would say it with period names.

2. 3,145,987   3 _million_, 145 _thousand_, 987

3. 30,123,500   30 _million_, 123 _thousand_, 500

4. 876,023,001   876 _million_, 23 _thousand_, 1

5. 2,033,343   _2_ million, _33_ thousand, _343_

6. 93,523,201   _93_ million, _523_ thousand, _201_

Write each number in standard form.

7. twenty-seven million, four hundred fifty-three thousand, one hundred thirty-one

   27,453,131

8. three hundred six million, twenty thousand, three hundred seventeen

   306,020,317

9. one million, one hundred thirty-one thousand, seven

   1,131,007

Mixed Applications

10. The distance from the sun to Mars is one hundred forty-one million miles. Write the distance in standard form.

    141,000,000 mi

11. The Astrodome seats 45,000 people. If 40,000 people attend a game, how many seats are empty?

    5,000 seats

Problem-Solving Strategy

Use a Table

For Exercises 1–3, use the table.

MOTOR VEHICLE PRODUCTION IN THE UNITED STATES AND JAPAN, 1950–1990		
Year	United States	Japan
1950	8,006,000	32,000
1960	7,905,000	482,000
1970	8,284,000	5,289,000
1980	8,010,000	11,043,000
1990	9,783,000	13,487,000

(handwritten margin notes: 7,974,000; 7,423,000; 2,995,000; 3,033,000; 3,704,000)

1. During which year was there the greatest difference in motor vehicle production between the United States and Japan?

   1950

2. By how much did production increase in Japan between 1950 and 1960?

   450000

3. During which years did Japan produce more vehicles than the United States?

   1990 + 1980

Mixed Applications

Solve.

CHOOSE A STRATEGY

• Use a Table   • Act It Out   • Make a Model   • Work Backward

4. Tony spent $5 to rent a bicycle and $3 for snacks. He found $1 and put it in his pocket. When he got home, he had $6 in his pocket. How much money did he begin with?

   $13

5. Four friends are in line to ride the bus. Julia is in front of Susan. Anne is between Susan and Carrie. Carrie is last in line. In what order are the friends in line?

   Julia, Susan, Anne, Carrie

Comparing on a Number Line

Use the number line to compare. Write < or >.

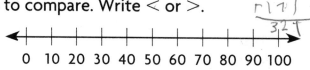

```
←+——+——+——+——+——+——+——+——+——+——+——→
  0  10 20 30 40 50 60 70 80 90 100
```

1. 10 $<$ 30　　2. 60 $<$ 90　　3. 80 $>$ 30　　4. 20 $<$ 60

```
←+——+——+——+——+——+——+——+——+——+——+——→
  0  100 200 300 400 500 600 700 800 900 1,000
```

5. 300 $<$ 400　　6. 900 $>$ 700　　7. 400 $<$ 700　　8. 400 $>$ 100

```
←+——+——+——+——+——+——+——+——+——+——+——→
  0  1,000 2,000 3,000 4,000 5,000 6,000 7,000 8,000 9,000
```

9. 1,000 $<$ 4,000　　10. 3,000 $>$ 2,000　　11. 4,000 $>$ 2,000

Compare the numbers and write < or >.

12. 400 $<$ 600　　13. 45 $<$ 47　　14. 460 $>$ 390　　15. 7,000 $>$ 4,000

Mixed Applications

16. Hana has 327 books on one large bookshelf. Her sister Yoko has 150 books on one bookshelf and 171 books on another bookshelf. Who has more books?

    Hana

17. Chet got home from school at 3:00. He worked on homework for 45 minutes and played basketball for 45 minutes. What time is it now?

    4:30

18. Explain why you would not use a number line marked with hundreds to compare the numbers 1,820 and 1,850.

19. The Eiffel Tower is 984 ft tall. The Leaning Tower of Pisa is 179 ft tall. Which building is taller?

    Eiffel Tower

    How much taller?

    805 ft ller

Name _Emily Emily_

Comparing Numbers

Write the greatest place-value position in which the digits are different.
Write the greater number.

1. 45, 48

ones

48

2. 56, 49

tens

56

3. 95, 59

tens

95

4. 251, 258

ones

258

5. 345, 401

hundreds

401

6. 461, 460

ones

461

7. 2,459; 2,468

tens

2,459

8. 4,821; 4,398

hundreds

4,821

Compare the numbers. Write the comparison, using <, >, or =.

9. 64
46

$64 > 46$

10. 165
174

$165 < 174$

11. 503
502

$503 > 502$

12. 98
98

$98 = 98$

Mixed Applications

For Problems 13–16, use the table.

13. Which team has the most points?

Dolphins

14. How many points do the Sharks need to earn in order to catch up with the Dolphins?

40 Points

SEMINOLE SWIM TEAMS	
Swim Team	**Points**
Dolphins	435
Sharks	395
Seals	415
Whales	400

15. If the Seals earn 50 points and the Dolphins earn 20 points, who will be ahead? By how much?

Seals 10 Points

16. There are 9 swimmers on each team. How many swimmers are there in all?

36 swimmers

Problem-Solving Strategy

Guess and Check

Guess and check to solve.

1. A movie ticket and popcorn cost $6. The ticket costs twice as much as the popcorn. How much does the ticket cost?

   _$4_____

2. The distance around a square table is 20 feet. What is the length of each side?

   _5 ft._____

3. The sum of two numbers is 30. Their difference is 2. What are the two numbers?

   _14 + 16_____

4. Bill has 6 coins that total $0.58. How many of each coin does he have?

   2 quarters, 1 nickle
   _3 pennies_____

Mixed Applications

Solve.

┌─────── **CHOOSE A STRATEGY** ───────┐

• **Make a Model** • **Act It Out** • **Guess and Check** • **Work Backward** • **Use a Table**

5. Maria has organized her bead collection in 3 boxes. Each box has 10 drawers, and each drawer has 10 beads. How many beads does Maria have?

   _300 beads_____

6. The school raised $1,000 during June and July. In June the school raised $200 more than in July. How much money did the school raise in June?

   _600_____

7. Tim spent half the money in his wallet for a kite. He won $4 in a kite-flying contest and put the money into his wallet. He now has $9. How much money did he have before he bought the kite?

   _$10_____

8. Four students are lining up in order of height. Alma is taller than Rosa. Pablo is shorter than Mario. Rosa's height is between Alma's and Mario's. List the students in order, beginning with the shortest.

   Pablo, Maria, Rosa
   _Alma_____

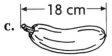

Ordering Numbers

Order from the least to the greatest length.

1. a. ├─20 cm─┤ 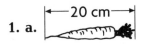 b. ├─13 cm─┤ c. ├─18 cm─┤

b, C, A _____

2. a. ├─150 mm─┤ b. ├─225 mm─┤ c. ├─190 mm─┤

A, C, b _____

Mixed Applications

For Problems 3–4, use the map.

3. Which city on the map is closer to Gardner?

   Roseburg _____

4. John lives in Bedford. He needs to do errands in Roseburg and in Gardner and then drive back home. What is the distance, in miles, of the shortest trip he can make?

   127 mi _____

5. Joey's and Rick's ages together are 18. Joey is 2 times as old as Rick.

   How old is Joey? ___12___

   How old is Rick? ___6___

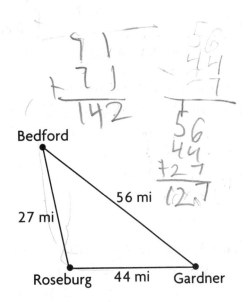

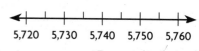

More About Ordering Numbers

Write the numbers in order from the least to the greatest.

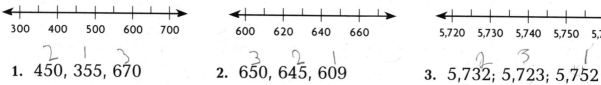

| 300 | 400 | 500 | 600 | 700 |

| 600 | 620 | 640 | 660 |

| 5,720 | 5,730 | 5,740 | 5,750 | 5,760 |

1. 450, 355, 670

355, 450, 670

2. 650, 645, 609

609, 645, 650

3. 5,732; 5,723; 5,752

5,752, 5,732, 5,723

Write the numbers in order from the greatest to the least.

4. 548, 648, 567

648, 567, 348

5. 413, 500, 431

500, 431, 413

6. 567, 923, 568

923, 568, 567

7. 2,645; 2,642; 2,671

2,671, 2,645, 2,642

8. 4,123; 4,145; 4,200

4,200, 4,145, 4,123

9. 7,504; 7,542; 7,540

7,504, 7,542, 7,540

Mixed Applications

For Problem 10, use the baseball season table.

10. Write in order the names of each player. Start with the least number of hits and end with the greatest number of hits.

Kyoko, jason, maya

BASEBALL SEASON HITS	
Player	Total Number of Hits
Jason	438
Maya	483
Kyoko	396

For Problems 11–12, use the tunnel table.

11. Which tunnel is the longest?

Holland Tunnel

12. How much longer is the Holland Tunnel than the Lincoln Tunnel?

341 moren

LONG TUNNELS	
Name of Tunnel	Length in Feet
Holland Tunnel	8,557 ft
Baltimore Harbor Tunnel	7,650 ft
Lincoln Tunnel	8,216 ft

Sorting and Comparing

Vocabulary

1. A _venn diagram_ uses circles to show relationships among different sets of things.

Place the numbers where they belong in each Venn diagram below.

2. 80, 6, 59, 74, 99, 40, 49, 77, 1

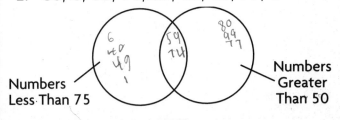

Numbers Less Than 75 — Numbers Greater Than 50

3. 145, 401, 940, 32, 856, 700

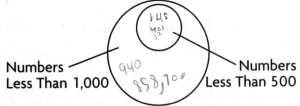

Numbers Less Than 1,000 — Numbers Less Than 500

4. Draw a Venn diagram for *Numbers Greater Than 2,000* and *Numbers Less Than 5,000*. Include 2,500; 7,000; 425; 3,500; 1,950; and 4,000.

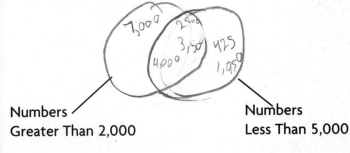

Numbers Greater Than 2,000 — Numbers Less Than 5,000

5. Make and label a Venn diagram comparing these numbers: 325, 675, 225, 650, 700, and 125.

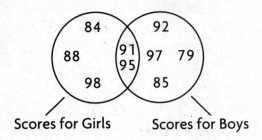

Greater than 100   Less than 200

Mixed Applications

For Problems 6–7, use the Venn diagram at the right.

6. Did a boy, a girl, or both get a score of 91? of 84?

   both, Girl

7. Did a boy or a girl get the highest score? Girl

Scores in Spelling Contest

84   92
88   91 95   97 79
98   85

Scores for Girls   Scores for Boys

Telling Time

Write the letter of the unit used to measure the time. Use each answer only once.

1. to take a shower   __C__

                                                    a. days

2. to drive across
the United States   __A__   b. hours

                                                    c. minutes

3. to button a button   __d__

                                                    d. seconds

4. to get a night's sleep   __b__

Write the time shown on the clock. Include seconds.

5.

1:40 and 25 sec.

6.

11:05 and 15 sec

7.

8:55 and 5 sec.

Write the time as shown on a digital clock.

8. 7 minutes past 3

3:07

9. 32 minutes past 10

10:32

10. 15 minutes past 5

5:15

11. 18 minutes past 2

2:18

12. 3 minutes past 12

12:03

13. 45 minutes past 6

6:45

Mixed Applications

14. Susan wakes up at 7:10 on school mornings. Draw the time as it would appear on an analog clock.

15. Mr. Johnson had 52 rakes in his store. After a sale, 8 rakes were left. How many rakes did Mr. Johnson sell?

44 rakes

A.M. and P.M.

Vocabulary

Complete.

1. _A.M._ means "before noon."

2. _P.M._ means "after noon."

3. A.M. and P.M. are not used with a _24-hour_ clock.

Write the time, using A.M. or P.M.

4. when the sun rises

_A.M._

5. when the sun sets

_P.M._

6. when you wake up

_A.M_

7. when the gas station closes

_P.M_

8. when you eat breakfast

_A.M_

9. when the library opens

_A.m._

Write the time as shown on a 24-hour clock.

10. 6:00 A.M.

_0600_

11. 2:00 P.M.

_1400_

12. 10:00 A.M.

_1000_

Write the time as shown on a 12-hour clock. Use A.M. or P.M.

13. 0200

_2:00 Am._

14. 0500

_5:00 A.m_

15. 1600

_4:00 P.m_

Mixed Applications

16. Kim went to a play that started at 7:30 P.M. Lee went to a play that started at 2000 hours. Whose play started earlier? Write the starting time of Lee's play, using A.M. or P.M.

8:00 P.m. Kim

17. It took Marc 25 minutes to wash his car. Then he worked 18 minutes to vacuum it and 90 minutes to wax it. How many minutes did he spend working on his car?

133 min.

Elapsed Time on a Clock

Vocabulary

Fill in the blank to complete the sentence.

1. ___Elapased Time___ is the time that passes
   from the start of an activity to the end of that activity.

Use an analog clock to find the elapsed time.

2. **start:** 7:30 A.M.
   end: 3:30 P.M.

   _8 hr_

3. **start:** 8:05 A.M.
   end: 9:55 A.M.

   1 hr 50 min

4. **start:** 9:15 P.M.
   end: 11:25 P.M.

   2 hr 10 min

Write the ending time.

5. **starting time:** 8:15 A.M.
   elapsed time: 3 hr 5 min

   _11:20 AM_

6. **starting time:** 9:05 A.M.
   elapsed time: 5 hr 45 min

   _2:50 pm_

Complete the table.

	Start Time	End Time	Elapsed Time
7.	7:20 A.M.	_8:50 Am_	1 hr 30 min
8.	10:20 A.M.	4:15 P.M.	_5 hr 55 min_

Mixed Applications

9. Max's school day begins at
   7:50 A.M. It ends at 2:20 P.M.
   How much time does Max
   spend at school each day?

   6 hr 30 min

10. Max bought a pencil for $0.10
    at the school store. He also
    bought a notebook for $0.89.
    What was his change from a
    $5.00 bill?

    _$4.01_

Using a Schedule

For Problems 1–3, use the schedule.

Saturday Storytelling Times at the Library	
10:00 A.M. *= 10:30*	"Beauty and the Beast"
10:45 A.M. *= 11:15*	"Jumanji"
11:45 A.M. *= 12:15*	"The Funny Little Woman"
1:15 P.M. *= 1:45*	"The Tin Soldier"

1. Each story lasts 30 minutes. At what time will each
   one end? _10:30, 11:15, 12:15, 1:45_

2. Jamal arrived at the library at 9:25 A.M. How long must
   he stay in order to hear two complete stories? _1 hr 5 a min._

3. How long a break did the librarian have between telling
   "The Funny Little Woman" and "The Tin Soldier"? _1 hr_

Mixed Applications

4. Tom wakes up at 6:55 A.M.
   Bill wakes up at 7:04 A.M.
   Who wakes up earlier? How
   much earlier?

   Tom 9 min.

5. Tom and Bill leave for school
   at 7:50 A.M. They arrive at
   8:05 A.M. How long does it take
   them to walk to school?

   15 min

6. The soccer team starts practice
   at 3:55 P.M. How much time
   does the team have to practice
   before the school bus arrives at
   4:50 P.M. to take them home?

   55 min.

7. Jill has put her models on a
   table that is 40 inches long.
   The perimeter of the table is
   120 inches. How wide is the
   table?

   20 inches

Problem-Solving Strategy

Make a Table

Complete the table to show John's summer work schedule.

1. During the summer John works at the snack bar on Mondays from 10:00 A.M. to noon. On Tuesdays and Thursdays, he works from 1:00 P.M. to 3:30 P.M. He works on Saturdays from 10:00 A.M. to 2:00 P.M.

Day	Start Time	End Time	Time Worked
Monday	10:00 A.M.	noon	2 hr
Tuesday	1:00 Pm.	3:30 Pm.	2hr 30min
Thursday	1:00 Pm	3:30 Pm	2hr 30min
Saturday	10:00 AM	2:00 Pm	4hr

For Problems 2 and 3, use the table.

2. How many hours does John work each week? __11 hr__

3. John rides to and from work on his bicycle. It takes him 15 minutes to ride each way. At what time does John arrive home from work on Thursdays?

   __3:45 Pm__

Mixed Applications

Solve.

┌─────── CHOOSE A STRATEGY ───────┐

• **Make a Model**   • **Act It Out**   • **Guess and Check**   • **Work Backward**

4. Julia built a small model airplane and a car in 2 hours. It took her 20 minutes longer to build the airplane than the car. How long did it take her to build each model?

   __Car 50min__

   __airplane 1hr and 10min__

5. Lita arrived at school at 8:35 A.M. Her bus ride took 15 minutes. She spent 5 minutes walking to the bus stop and 5 minutes waiting for the bus. At what time did Lita leave her house?

   __8:10 AM__

Elapsed Time on a Calendar

For Problems 1–3, use the calendars.

Camp Windy	
Session 1:	Jul 13–Jul 17
Session 2:	Jul 27–Jul 31
Session 3:	Aug 3–Aug 14

June						
Sun	Mon	Tue	Wed	Thu	Fri	Sat
	1	2	3	4	5	6
7	8	9	10	11	12	13
14	15	16	17	18	19	20
21	22	23	24	25	26	27
28	29	30				

July						
Sun	Mon	Tue	Wed	Thu	Fri	Sat
			1	2	3	4
5	6	7	8	9	10	11
12	13	14	15	16	17	18
19	20	21	22	23	24	25
26	27	28	29	30	31	

August						
Sun	Mon	Tue	Wed	Thu	Fri	Sat
						1
2	3	4	5	6	7	8
9	10	11	12	13	14	15
16	17	18	19	20	21	22
23	24	25	26	27	28	29
30	31					

1. The camp director bought art supplies 4 weeks before the beginning of the first session of camp. On what date did she buy art supplies?

   June 15

2. In Session 3, the campers put on a puppet show on the second Wednesday of the session. What was the date of the puppet show?

   August 12

3. Jim plans to attend Session 2 of camp. His last day of school is June 19. About how many weeks of summer vacation will Jim have before camp begins?

   5 weeks

Mixed Applications

4. Brenda takes blood samples from a patient every 45 minutes. She takes the first sample at 10:15 A.M. and the last sample at 1:15 P.M. How many samples does she take?

   5 samples

5. Randy's Sports Store sold 23 baseball gloves in May. In June the store sold 35 baseball gloves. How many more baseball gloves were sold in June than in May?

   12 more

Organizing Data in Tables

Vocabulary

Complete the sentence.

1. The numbers in the ___cumulative frequency___
column show the sum as each new line of data is entered.

For Exercises 2–3, use the frequency table.

FROZEN POPS SOLD		
Day	**Number of Frozen Pops**	**Cumulative Frequency**
Monday	15	15
Tuesday	24	39
Wednesday	19	58
Thursday	9	67
Friday	21	88

2. The cumulative frequency for Wednesday is __58__.
This is the sum of the numbers in the frequency column
for which days?

___Mon.___, ___Tues.___, and ___Wed.___.

3. How many frozen pops in all were sold on Monday and Tuesday?

___39___

Mixed Applications

For Problems 4–5, use the frequency table.

4. How many more people attended
Game 2 than Game 1?

___55 people___

5. Which game had the fewest
people?

___gam 3___

NUMBER OF PEOPLE AT HOME GAMES	
Game	**Number of People**
1	140
2	195
3	116
4	204

Organizing Data

Ben made this table to organize
the results of an experiment. He
spun a three-color spinner and
a three-number spinner. Ben's first
outcome was spinning blue and
spinning the number 1.

EXPERIMENT RESULTS			
	Red	Yellow	Blue
1	/	///	//
2	///		‖‖
3	//	//	//

For Exercises 1–4, use the table.

1. What are the possible outcomes
for this experiment?

red1, Red2, Red3

yellow1, yellow2, yellow3

Blue1, Blue2, Blue3

2. How many times did Ben spin
the color red and the number 2
at the same time?

3

3. Which outcome happened the
most often in Ben's experiment?

Blue2

4. How many possible outcomes
would there be if Ben used a
four-color spinner?

12

Mixed Applications

5. It took Ben 15 minutes to make
his spinner, 5 minutes to make
his table, and 10 minutes to do
his experiment. Ben began
working at 10:10 A.M. When did
he complete his experiment?

10:40AM

6. You toss a coin and a two-
colored counter that is red
on one side and yellow on
the other. What are the
possible outcomes?

heads red, heads yellow,
tails red, tails yellow

7. The pet shop has 24 bags of cat
food. The shop uses 3 bags each
day. How many days will the
cat food last?

8 Days

8. Four students ran a race. Joe
finished after Sally. Edith
finished before Joe but after
Gerry. Who finished last?

Joe

Problem-Solving Strategy

Make an Organized List

Make an organized list to solve.

1. Don is making a wooden box at camp. He can make a small, medium, or large box. He can use cedar or pine. How many different boxes can Don choose to make?

   6 Boxes

2. Carrie packs 3 shirts and 2 pairs of pants for a camping trip. The shirts are white, red, and green. The pants are black and blue. How many different outfits can she wear?

   6 outfits

3. Carlos wants to take a pottery class or a drawing class after school. Pottery and drawing classes are taught Monday, Tuesday, Wednesday, and Thursday afternoons. How many class and day combinations are there?

   8 combos.

4. Anne can choose one flavor of ice cream and one topping. The ice cream flavors are vanilla, chocolate, and strawberry. The toppings are nuts, candies, and whipped cream. How many combinations are there?

   9 combos.

Mixed Applications

Solve.

CHOOSE A STRATEGY

• Act It Out • Make a Model • Write a Number Sentence • Make an Organized List

5. For lunch Ken may order a sandwich with chicken, turkey, or tuna. He can have the sandwich on white bread or whole wheat bread. How many choices does he have?

   6 choices

6. Hilda's quilt design has 7 rows of squares. There are 5 squares in each row. How many squares are there in all?

   35 squares

7. Bill has 8 coins that total $0.84. Three of the coins are quarters. What are the rest of the coins?

   _1 n, 4 p_

8. Paula buys a 90-minute tape for $2.49 and a 60-minute tape. The total is $4.48. How much is the 60-minute tape?

   _$1.99_

Understanding Surveys

Vocabulary

Complete the sentence.

1. James wanted to know which subject each classmate likes best. He asked several people the same question

   and took a __Survey__.

Mr. Whitman made a survey to find out which fruits people liked best. He asked, "Is your favorite fruit apples, bananas, oranges, or pears?" The table shows the results of his survey.

FAVORITE FRUITS	
Fruit	**Votes**
Apples	HHT IIII
Bananas	IIII
Oranges	HHT II
Pears	II

For Problems 2–5, use the table.

2. What type of fruit was chosen by the most students?

   __apples__

3. How many students took part in the survey?

   __22 students__

4. How do you think the survey results would have been different if Mr. Whitman had asked, "What is your favorite fruit?"

   __there would be more__
   __fruits listed.__

5. Explain why this statement may not be true: Two students in Mr. Whitman's survey like pears better than any other fruit.

   __there favorite fruit__
   __might not be that fruit.__

Mixed Applications

6. Katrina can have turkey or cheese. She can have white bread or wheat bread. What sandwiches could she have?

   __wheat bread/Turky/__
   __wheat bread/cheese/__
   __white bread/Turky/__
   __white bread/Cheese__

7. Janet has 36 British and French stamps in her collection. She has 3 times as many British stamps as French stamps. How many of the stamps are British?

   __27 British__

Comparing Graphs

Vocabulary

Complete the sentence.

1. The distance between the numbers of a graph is called

the _interval_ .

For Exercises 2–5, use the graphs below.

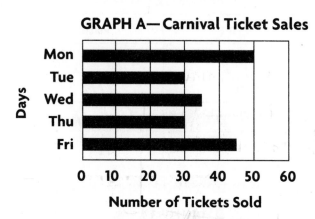

GRAPH A—Carnival Ticket Sales

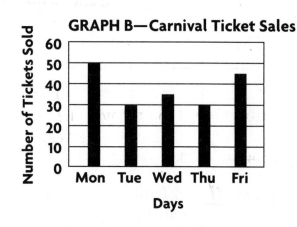

GRAPH B—Carnival Ticket Sales

2. How are Graphs A and B different?

one is horizontal and
ond is vertical

3. How are Graphs A and B alike?

they have the same
data

4. What other interval could be used that would make the data easy to read?

+5 cy count

5. On which day were the most tickets sold?

Mon.

Mixed Applications

6. What intervals on the scale could you use for this set of data about the heights of plants in centimeters: 10, 14, 16, 20, 13, 18?

_2_

7. Ruth arrived at the carnival at 9:15 A.M. and stayed until 2:30 P.M. How much time did she spend at the carnival?

_5:15_

More About Comparing Graphs

Vocabulary

Complete the sentence.

1. The __scale__ is the series of numbers placed at fixed distances on the side of a graph.

For Exercises 2–4, use the graph.

2. What is the interval of the scale in the graph at the right?

   5s

3. Describe how the bars in the graph would look if you made a new graph, using a scale with intervals of 10.

   smaller

4. How would the bars change in the graph if the interval were 1?

   longer

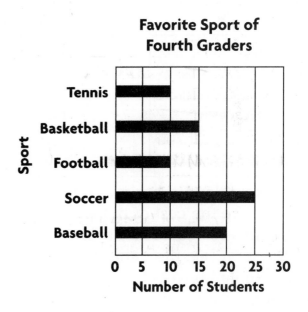

Favorite Sport of Fourth Graders

Sport: Tennis, Basketball, Football, Soccer, Baseball
Number of Students: 0 5 10 15 20 25 30

Mixed Applications

5. Suppose the scale of a bar graph is 0, 4, 8, 12, 16, 20. How would you draw a bar on this graph to represent the number 10?

   The bar would be between 8 and 12.

6. Molly bought 4 balloons for $0.50 each. She bought popcorn for $1.50. How much money did she spend? Molly paid with a $5 bill. How much change did she receive?

   $3.50, $1.50

7. A baker can make 8 batches of cookies in an hour. How many batches of cookies can the baker make in 7 hours?

   56 batches

8. Kip has a scarf. It has a red stripe, a blue stripe, and a white stripe. This pattern repeats. What color is the eighth stripe?

   blue

Exploring Double-Bar Graphs

Vocabulary

Complete the sentence.

1. A ___Double, bar graphs___ is used to compare similar kinds of data.

Bulbs (per package of 25)		
Bulbs	**Kevin's Flowers**	**Hillside Nursery**
Daffodil	$18.00	$14.00
Tulip	$10.00	$12.00
Hyacinth	$21.00	$12.00
Crocus	$5.00	$7.00

2. Make a double-bar graph to compare the cost of bulbs at Kevin's Flowers and at Hillside Nursery. Use the data from the table above. Choose an appropriate scale. Include a title, labels, a scale, and a key for both stores.

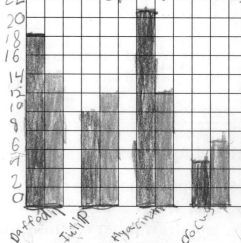

Mixed Applications

3. Tim conducted a survey to find out the favorite games played by first and sixth graders. He asked students to choose among the games wall ball, four square, soccer, and around the world. What kind of graph would be appropriate for this data? Explain.

___Double, bar graphs.___

_____

4. A group of 48 children are going on a picnic. Fruit juice comes 8 boxes to a pack. How many packs would give each child 2 fruit juice drinks?

___12 packs___

Reading a Line Graph

Vocabulary

Complete the sentence.

1. A _line graph_ uses a line to show how something changes over a period of time.

Joyce made this line graph to show the number of pages she read each day in a mystery book. For Problems 2–5, use the graph.

2. On what day did Joyce read the most pages? the fewest pages?

   Fri., mon.

3. How many pages did Joyce read on Thursday?

   15 pages

4. On which two days did Joyce read the same number of pages?

   Wed., Tue.

5. How many more pages did Joyce read on Friday than on Monday?

   15 more

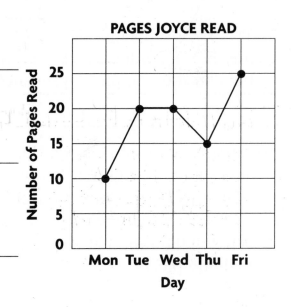

PAGES JOYCE READ

Number of Pages Read

Mon Tue Wed Thu Fri
Day

Mixed Applications

6. Simone is making a line graph with intervals of 4 on the scale. Her data include the numbers 5, 12, 8, 4, 29, and 20. Which numbers are graphed between the numbers on the scale?

   5, 5, Smant

7. Sandy read 3 pages on Monday. For the next 3 days she read twice as many pages as she read the day before. How many pages did she read in all?

   45 pages

Line Plot

Vocabulary

Complete the sentences.

1. A _Line plot_ is a diagram that shows the frequency of data.

2. The difference between the greatest and the least numbers

   in a set of data is called the _range_ .

For Problems 3–5, use the line plot at the right.

3. The X's on this line plot represent the number of students. What do the numbers on the line plot represent?

   The number of children add family

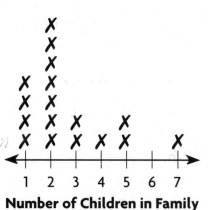

Number of Children in Family

4. What number of children do more students have in their families?

   2 children

5. What is the range of numbers used in this line plot?

   _6_

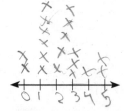

Slices of Pizza Eaten at a Party

Use the data in the table to complete the line plot.

Slices of Pizza Eaten at a Party						
Number of Slices	0	1	2	3	4	5
Number of Students	//	＃＃ /	＃＃	///	/	//

Mixed Applications

6. Use the data in the table. How many students attended the party?

   19 students

7. A group of athletes traveled to the pool in 5 vans. Each van held 8 athletes and one driver. How many people went to the pool?

   45 athletes

Stem-and-Leaf Plot

Vocabulary

Complete the sentences.

1. A __stem-and-leaf plot__ shows groups of data organized by place value.

2. The __mode__ is the number that occurs most often in a set of data.

3. The __median__ is the middle number in an ordered set of numbers.

The stem-and-leaf plot below shows the scores that fourth-grade students made in a spelling contest. For Problems 4–6, use the stem-and-leaf plot.

4. What are the least and the greatest scores?

   68, 95

5. What is the mode of the contest scores?

   88

6. What is the median of the contest scores?

   86

Spelling Scores

Stem	Leaves
6	8 8 9 9
7	2 3 5 5 6
8	4 4 6 7 8 8 8
9	1 2 2 3 4 5 5

Mixed Applications

7. Mr. Hall made a list of the heights in inches of the children at his family reunion. The heights are 42, 42, 44, 45, 47, 47, 49, 50, 50, 52, 52, 53, 56, 56, 57, 59, 60, 60, 62, 62, 62. Show these heights on a stem-and-leaf plot.

8. Students recorded how many seconds they took to complete a maze. The times in seconds were 14, 14, 15, 17, 19, 20, 24, 27, 27, 31, 33. Make a stem-and-leaf plot showing this data.

Choosing a Graph

Write the graph or plot you would choose to display data for each
of the following.

1. to show a record of a baby's
weight for six months

   _____line_____graph_____

2. to show how many bicycles
were sold each month at a store

   _____bar graph_____

3. to find the median age of the
teachers at a school

   ____stem-and-leaf___graph____

4. to compare the favorite sports of
boys and girls in your class

   ____2 bar graph_____

Explain why each graph or plot is not the best choice for
the data it shows. Tell which type of graph or plot would
be a better choice.

5. **DAILY HIGH TEMPERATURES FOR
SEPT. 15–21**

X X X X X X X
65 66 67 68 69 70 71

_____

_____

_____

6. **FAVORITE GAMES AT RECESS**

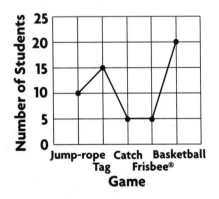

_____

_____

_____

_____

_____

Mixed Applications

7. Maria wants to make a graph
to compare the weights of four
different wild cats. What graph
will best display Maria's data?

   _____bar graph_____

8. Jackie needs 32 feet of fencing
to enclose her vegetable garden.
The length of the garden is 10
feet. How wide is the garden?

   _____6 feet_____

Problem-Solving Strategy

Make a Graph

Make a graph or plot for each table.

1.   **Pencils in Each Student's Desk**

Number of Pencils	Number of Students
0	5
1	7
2	4
3	4
4	1

2.   **Favorite Music**

Music Choices	Number of Students
Classical	4
Jazz	3
Folk	7
Rock and Roll	6

Mixed Applications

Solve.

CHOOSE A STRATEGY

- **Make an Organized List**
- **Guess and Check**
- **Make a Graph**
- **Work Backward**

3. Make a graph or plot to show high temperatures for 13 cities in the United States. The temperatures were 80, 79, 76, 91, 89, 84, 78, 80, 82, 90, 79, 79, 85.

4. Jim has twice as many coins in his pocket as Hans. Together they have between 15 and 20 coins. How many coins might Hans have?

_____

Certain and Impossible

Vocabulary

Fill in the blank.

1. If the event will always happen, it is _certain_.

2. If the event is _impossible_, it will never happen.

3. When you tell what will happen in an experiment, you _predict_.

Tell if each event is certain or impossible. Write *certain* or *impossible*.

4. getting orange paint when you mix blue paint with white paint

impossible

5. picking a number that ends in a 5 or a 0 from a set of cards with the multiples of 5 from 5 to 50

certain

For Exercises 6 and 7, use the cards below.

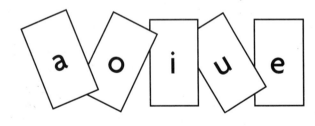

6. Is choosing a card with the letter z certain or impossible?

impossible

7. Is it certain or impossible that you will choose a card with a vowel?

certain

Mixed Applications

8. Evita has four items in a drawer: a red jersey, a green sweater, purple shorts, and a black sweatshirt. Is it certain or impossible that she will pull out a striped top from the drawer?

impossible

9. Colin makes a spinner with three sections and numbers them 3, 4, and 5. If he spins twice and multiplies the two numbers, what are all the products he could get?

_9, 12, 15, 16, 20, 25,_

Likely and Unlikely

Vocabulary

1. What is the name for something that happens in an

   experiment that brings about an outcome? ___event___

For Problems 2–3, tell whether each event is *likely* or *unlikely*.

2. having the same birthday as 5 other classmates ___unlikely___

3. eating a piece of fruit—or some food with fruit in it—today ___likely___

Look at the set of cards and spinner.

4. If you pick a card 10 times without looking, replacing the card each time, which number are you unlikely to pick? Why?

   ___1_____

5. Which letter on the spinner are you likely to spin the most

   in 10 spins? Explain. ___A_____

   _____

Mixed Applications

6. Lyndon is putting 10 marbles in a bag. He has red, blue, green, and black marbles. He wants to make pulling a red, green, or black marble unlikely and pulling a blue marble likely. How many of each color should he put in the bag?

   ___5 blue, 2 green, 2 red___

   ___1 black___

7. Chelsea has 4 T-shirts and 2 pairs of shorts that she can wear to exercise class. How many different outfits can she wear to class?

   ___8 outfits___

Predicting Outcomes

Vocabulary

Write the word or phrase that means the same thing.

1. possible ways _Out comes_____

2. has the same chance of happening _equally likely_____

Make a six-section spinner for an experiment. You may use colors, numbers, or shapes in the sections. Make your spinner so that it has likely outcomes as well as other possible outcomes.

First, spin 15 times and record the results in the tally table. Spin 30 more times and record the results in the other tally table. Then, answer Exercise 3.

SPINNER EXPERIMENT—15 SPINS	
Outcome	Tallies

SPINNER EXPERIMENT—30 SPINS	
Outcome	Tallies

3. Did the likely outcomes happen more often than the other possible outcomes in the 15-spin experiment or

in the 30-spin experiment? _____

Mixed Applications

4. RaeAnn put some green marbles, 4 red marbles, 2 purple marbles, and 5 blue marbles in a bag. She counted 14 marbles in the bag in all. How many green marbles did she put in the bag?

5. Phil made a spinner. In the 6 sections, he drew an orange circle, a red circle, a blue circle, a red triangle, a blue triangle, and a blue square. Is spinning a blue shape a likely outcome? Explain.

_____

_____

Probability

Vocabulary

Fill in the blank.

1. _pobability_ is the chance that an event will happen.

___

Look at the spinner at the right. Find the probability of spinning each.

2. the letter C __$\frac{1}{5}$__

3. the letter E __$\frac{1}{5}$__

4. a vowel __$\frac{2}{5}$__

5. a letter in the word _cab_ __$\frac{3}{5}$__

Look at the cards at the right. Find the probability of choosing each if you were to choose without looking.

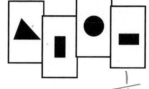

6. a circle __$\frac{1}{4}$__

7. a triangle __$\frac{1}{4}$__

8. a rectangle __$\frac{2}{4}$__

9. a shape with straight sides __$\frac{3}{4}$__

For Problems 10 and 11, use the spinner below.

10. What is the probability of spinning the number 1 or 2? __$\frac{4}{6}$__

11. What is the probability of spinning a number less than 5? __$\frac{6}{6}$__

Mixed Applications

12. A number cube is labeled with the numbers 3, 6, 9, 12, 15, and 18. Describe an outcome of rolling the cube that has a probability of $\frac{3}{6}$, or $\frac{1}{2}$.

less than ten

13. At the marble factory, every third marble down the assembly line has glitter inside it. Every fifth marble has a stripe in it. Do more marbles have glitter or stripes?

glitter

Testing for Fairness

Vocabulary

Fill in the blank.

1. ___Fairness___ of a game is when one player is not more likely to win than another.

Tell if each spinner is fair. Write *yes* or *no*. If your answer is *no*, explain.

2.

___yes___

_____

3.

___no___

_____

In Victor's game, players choose to be either "2" or "3." Players take turns rolling a number cube labeled 1 to 6. If a player is a "2" and rolls a 2, 4, or 6, he or she scores a point. If a player is a "3" and rolls a 3 or a 6, he or she gets a point.

4. What is the probability of rolling the numbers 2, 4, or 6? the numbers 3 or 6? $\frac{3}{6}$ $\frac{2}{6}$

_____

5. Why is this game not fair?

_____

_____

Mixed Applications

6. Leslie and Melanie started walking home from school at 3:20. It takes Leslie 15 minutes to reach home. It takes Melanie 10 more minutes than Leslie to reach home. At what time did each girl arrive home?

L 3:35, M 3:45

7. Oscar is making a spinner that has 6 equal sections. How can he use the colors yellow, green, and blue to color the spinner so that there is an equal chance of spinning each one?

_____

_____

Name _____

Problem-Solving Strategy

Make a Model

Make a model to solve.

1. Tara is completing a spinner that has been divided into 6 sections. Two of the sections are each $\frac{1}{4}$ of the spinner. Four of the sections are each $\frac{1}{8}$ of the spinner. If Tara uses 3 colors and paints each section 1 color, will her spinner be fair? Explain.

_no_

_____

_____

2. Nevin's spinner is divided into 10 equal sections. Every fifth section is blue. The section before each blue section is yellow. The section after each blue section is green. Half of the remaining sections are purple, and the rest are red. Is Nevin's spinner fair? Explain.

yes

_____

Mixed Applications

Solve.

CHOOSE A STRATEGY

• Make a Graph   • Guess and Check   • Use a Table   • Make a Model   • Act It Out

3. A game board has 24 squares for players to land on between *Start* and *Finish*. Every fourth square is labeled *Bonus Card*. Every sixth square is labeled *Extra Turn*. Which squares have both labels?

_12, 24_

_____

5. What kind of graph would be best for showing the data from the table at the right?

_____

4. Tika pulled some quarters, dimes, and nickels out of her pocket. She counted 8 coins. The coins totaled $1.15. How many of each coin did she have?

_Q3, D3, N2_

POPULATION GROWTH IN ACTION	
Year	Population
1975	13,759
1985	21,461
1995	24,568

Name _____

Exploring Geometric Figures

Vocabulary

Write the letter of the phrase that describes how each figure can
be measured.

1. __B__ one-dimensional figure   a. measured in cubic units

2. __C__ two-dimensional figure   b. measured in linear units

3. __A__ three-dimensional figure   c. measured in square units

---

Write *one-dimensional, two-dimensional,* or *three-dimensional* to
describe each figure.

4.
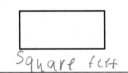
__1-d__

5.
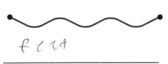
__3-d__

6.

__2-d__

Choose *feet, square feet,* or *cubic feet* to measure each.

7.

__Cubic ft__

8.

__Square feet__

9.

__feet__

10.

__Cubic ft__

11.
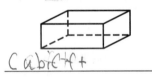
__feet__

12.

__cubic ft__

13.

__Square feet__

14.

__Square feet__

15.

__Cubic ft__

Mixed Applications

16. Bitsy and Ribbons both eat a cup
of dog food each day. How much
dog food do they eat in a week?

__14 cups__

17. Explain why a refrigerator is
measured in cubic feet.

__it's 3-d__

Patterns for Solid Figures

Vocabulary

Fill in the blank.

1. A __net__ is a two-dimensional pattern of a three-dimensional figure.

Write the letter of the figure that is made with each net.

2.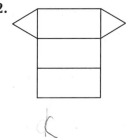

_c_

3.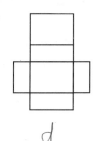

_d_

4.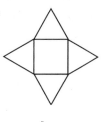

_A_

5.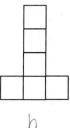

_b_

a.

b.

c.

d.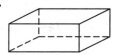

6. Which of the following nets would make a rectangular prism?

_b_   _d_

_____

a.

b.

c.

d.

Mixed Applications

7. Martina wants to make a three-dimensional model of the pyramids at Giza. The pyramids have a square base and 4 triangular sides. Draw the net she needs to make for the pyramid.

8. A high school starts at 7:30 A.M. Students have two 1-hour classes, a 30-minute homeroom period, and then another 1-hour class before lunch. What time is lunch?

_11:00 A.M._

Faces of Solid Figures

Vocabulary

Fill in the blank.

1. A ___vertex___ is a corner where three sides meet in a solid figure.

2. ___vertices___ are more than one vertex.

Write the names of the plane figures that are the faces of each three-dimensional figure.

3.
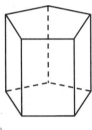

___pentagon, rectangles___

4.
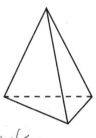

___triangle___

Write the names of the faces and the number of each face on the three-dimensional figure.

5. cube

___6 squares___

6. triangular pyramid

___4 triangles___

7. pentagonal prism

___2 pentagons, 5 rectangles___

8. triangular prism

___3 rectangles, 2 triangles___

9. square pyramid

___4 triangles, 1 square___

10. rectangular prism

___6 rectangles___

Mixed Applications

11. A cereal box is in the shape of a rectangular prism. How many faces does it have? What is the shape of each face?

   ___6 faces, rectangle,___

12. Jennifer drives 16 miles to work. She drives home along the same route. How far does Jennifer drive in 2 days?

   ___64 miles___

More About Solid Figures

Complete the table by finding the faces, vertices, and edges of the figures.

	Figure	Name of Figure	Number of Faces	Number of Vertices	Number of Edges
1.		Cube	6	8	12
2.		Triangular pyramid	4	4	6
3.		Triangular prism	5	6	9
4.		Square pyramid	5	5	8
5.		Rectangular prism	6	8	12

Write the letter of the figure that answers each question.

6. Which figure has more faces?

   __B__

   a. a triangular prism
   b. a rectangular prism

7. Which figure has fewer

   vertices? __A__

   a. a triangular pyramid
   b. a triangular prism

8. Which figure has the fewest

   edges? __A__

   a. a triangular pyramid
   b. a square pyramid

9. Which figure has more sets of

   congruent faces? __B__

   a. a triangular prism
   b. a rectangular prism

Mixed Applications

10. I am a three-dimensional figure with 6 faces, 8 vertices, 12 edges, and at least 4 rectangular faces. What am I?

    __Rectangular prism__

11. There are 215 seats in a movie theater. A movie is shown 4 times a day. If all the seats are filled, how many people see the movie in a day?

    __860 people__

Name _____

Plane Figures on a Coordinate Grid

Vocabulary

Fill in the blanks.

1. The numbers in an ___ordered pair___ represent the number of
   spaces you move to the right and up to locate a point on the grid.

Write the ordered pairs used to make each plane figure.

2.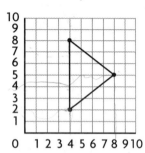

(4,2), (4,8),
(8,5)

3.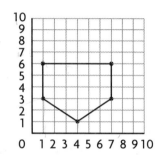

4,13, (1,3)(1,6),
(7,6), (7,3)

4.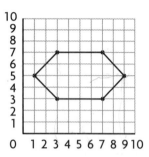

(3,7), (3,1),
4,5),(7,7),(7,1),
(9,5)

Mark the ordered pairs on the grids below. Draw a figure with vertices at
the named points. Write the name of the figure.

5. (2,2), (7,2), (5,5)

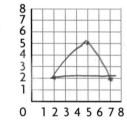

__triangle__

6. (1,2), (1,5), (6,5), (6,2)

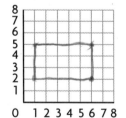

__rectangle__

7. (1,3), (3,1), (5,1),(5,5), (3,5)

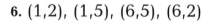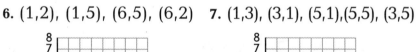

__pentagon__

Mixed Applications

8. Juan bought 4 boxes of 24 tiles
   each to make a floor design. He
   used all but 7 tiles. How many
   tiles did Juan use for the floor
   design?

   __89 tiles__

9. Toni was in the drugstore for
   15 minutes. She bought a brush
   for $2.75, 2 combs for $0.50
   each, and a bottle of shampoo
   for $1.75. How much did she
   spend in all?

   __$5.50__

Classifying and Sorting Solid Figures

Vocabulary

Write the letter of the corresponding solid figure.

1. _D_ cone

2. _A_ rectangular prism

3. _F_ triangular prism

4. _H_ cube

5. _E_ sphere

6. _B_ cylinder

7. _G_ square pyramid

8. _C_ triangular pyramid

a.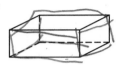

b.

c.

d.

e.

f.

g.

h.

Sort solid figures a.–h. into Venn diagrams. Write the letter of the appropriate solids in the diagrams below.

9.   6 Edges or Fewer   6 Edges or More

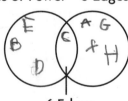

6 Edges

10.   Flat Faces   Curved Surfaces

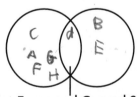

Flat Faces and Curved Surfaces

Mixed Applications

11. Use two solid figures to draw a model of a house.

12. Which solid figures would you choose?

    cube, square pyramid
    _____

Draw a Model

Name _____

Problem-Solving Strategy

Make an Organized List

Make an organized list to solve.

1. Inside Mark's desk are pencils, pens, erasers, a hand-
   ball, markers, a book, a box of crayons, and an apple.
   Sort the objects by their shape.

Box-Shaped	Cylinder-Shaped	Sphere-Shaped
erasers	pencils	ball
book	pens	apple
box crayons	markers	

2. The sports closet has baseballs, baseball bats, tumbling
   mats, basketballs, cans of tennis balls, and a balance
   beam. Sort the objects by their shape.

Sphere-Shaped	Box-Shaped	Cylinder-Shaped
baseball	t-mat	b-bat
b-ball	b-beam	tennis balls

3. Use the digits 2, 7, and 9. List all the three-digit numbers you
   can make without repeating any digits in the same number.

   279, 972, 729, 792, 297, 927

Mixed Applications

Solve.

┌─ **CHOOSE A STRATEGY** ─┐

- **Guess and Check** • **Make an Organized List** • **Work Backward** • **Act It Out**

4. Helen, Laura, and Aber had a
   bake sale. At the end of the
   day, they shared their money.
   They had 1 five-dollar bill, 2
   one-dollar bills, 6 quarters, and
   1 nickel. How much did each
   person receive?

   $2.85

5. Hannah spent $3 on a magazine.
   Then she spent $9 on a CD and
   $2 on a snack. Hannah had $12
   left after that. How much did she
   have to begin with?

   $26.00

Line Segments

Vocabulary

Write the letter of the word that best describes each phrase.

1. __D__   The shortest distance between two points on a line.

2. __E__   Line segments that never cross. They are always the same distance apart.

3. __C__   A flat surface with no end. Named by any three points.

4. __B__   A straight path in a plane with no end. Named by any two points on a line.

5. __A__   Identifies a location on an object and in space.

A. point

B. line

C. plane

D. line segment

E. parallel

Write *points, line, line segment,* or *plane* to name each figure.

F   G   H   I   J   K

6. __points__   7. __line segment__   8. __line__

Decide if the figure is a line segment. Write *yes* or *no*.

9. __no__   10. __yes__   11. __no__

Write *yes* or *no* to tell if the pair of line segments is parallel.

12. __no__   13. __no__   14. __yes__

Mixed Applications

15. A baseball diamond has 4 bases. Think of each base as a point. How many line segments are in a baseball runner's path?

__4 lines segments__

16. Nadeem buys 5 books priced at $3.99 each. Ann buys the same 5 books for $3.69 each. How much less money does Ann pay?

__$1.50__

Exploring Angles and Line Relationships

Vocabulary

Fill in the blanks.

1. A _ray_ is part of a line and has one endpoint.

2. When two rays have the same endpoint, they form an _angle_.

3. A _right_ angle forms a square corner.

4. An _acute_ angle is *less than* a right angle.

5. An _obtuse_ angle is *greater than* a right angle.

Write the name of each figure.

D

M   N

E   D

6. _point_

7. _line_

8. _ray_

Write *acute, right,* or *obtuse* to name each angle.

9. _obtuse_

10. _right_

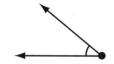

11. _acute_

12. _acute_

13. _right_

14. _obtuse_

Mixed Applications

15. Lily and Nasira are making 25 bracelets for the Soccer Team Raffle. Each hour, Lily can make 1 bracelet and Nasira can make $1\frac{1}{2}$ bracelets. How many hours will it take them to make 25 bracelets?

10 hours

16. Ben noticed a display in the supermarket. Each side was the same size, and every angle was the same. What type of angle was used?

acute

More About Angles and Line Relationships

Vocabulary

Fill in the blanks.

1. _intersecting_ lines are lines that cross each other.

2. _perpendicular_ lines intersect to form four right angles.

Write *intersecting*, *parallel*, or *perpendicular* to name each line relationship.

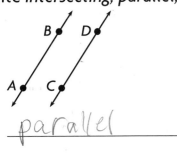

parallel

3. _____

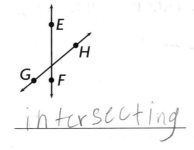

intersecting

4. _____

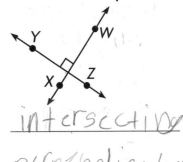

intersecting

5. _perpendicular_

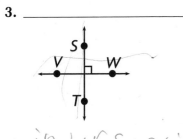

intersecting

6. _perpendicular_

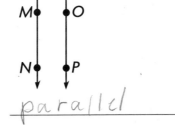

parallel

7. _____

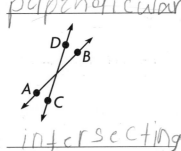

intersecting

8. _____

Mixed Applications

For Problems 9–11, use the map below.

9. Name the streets that intersect Winter Street.

   Season Road

   Fall Street

10. Name the streets that are parallel.

   sping, summer,

   winter

11. Name the type of angle created by the intersection of Winter Street and Fall Street.

   right

Exploring Circles

Vocabulary

Define the following words.

1. radius: A line segment from the center to any point on the circle

2. diameter: A line segment that passes through the center and has its endpoints on the circle

For Problems 3–6, use Circle 1.

3. The center of the circle is point __F__.

4. The diameter of the circle is line segment __GH__.

5. The radius of the circle is line segment __FI__,

   __FH__, __FJ__, or __FG__.

6. The points on the circle are __I__, __H__, __J__; and __G__.

7. Draw a circle. Label the center point A.
   Draw a radius AB. Draw a diameter CD.

For Problems 8–9, use Circles 2 and 3.

8. Name the center of each circle. __R, W__

9. Name each radius. __BS, RW, RT, WX,__

   __WY, WZ__

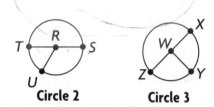

Circle 2   Circle 3

Mixed Applications

10. A round pizza was sliced into
    10 pieces. How many diameter
    cuts were needed?

    __5 dc__

11. Maria spent $12 for a pen and
    a book. The pen cost 3 times as
    much as the book. How much
    did each item cost?

    __$3, $9__

Polygons

Vocabulary

Write the letter of the figure that has the same number of sides.

1. 5 sides _P_   2. 8 sides _A_   **A.** octagon   **B.** quadrilateral

3. 3 sides _E_   4. 6 sides _C_   **C.** hexagon   **D.** pentagon

5. 4 sides _B_   **E.** triangle

Complete the sentence.

6. A _polygon_ is a closed plane figure with straight sides.

Write *yes* or *no* to tell if the figure is a polygon.

7. _no_ 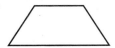   8. _yes_   9. _no_   10. _yes_

Name each polygon. Identify the number of sides.

11. 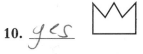   12. 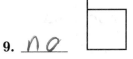   13.   14.

quadrilateral   _pentagon_   _octagon_   _hexagon_

_4_   _5_   _8_   _6_

Mixed Applications

15. Emma has twice as many stickers as Karina. Sarah has 8 more stickers than Karina. Amanda has 5 fewer stickers than Sarah. Amanda has 10 stickers. Who has the most stickers?

    Sarah

16. The Pentagon building in Arlington, Virginia, houses the U.S. Department of Defense. How many sides and angles do the outer walls of the Pentagon building have?

    _5 s, 5 a_

Quadrilaterals

Vocabulary

Fill in the blanks.

1. General _quadrilaterals_ have 4 sides and 4 angles.

2. _trapezoids_ have 2 sides that are parallel.

3. _parallelogram_ have 2 pairs of parallel sides. They have 2 of the same-size acute angles and 2 of the same-size obtuse angles.

4. A _rhombus_ has 4 equal sides. Its opposite sides are parallel and it has no right angles.

Name the kind of quadrilateral.

5.
rhombus

6.
parallogram

7.
trapezoid

8.
square

Draw the quadrilateral.

9. trapezoid

10. square

11. rhombus

12. parallelogram

13. rectangle

14. general quadrilateral

Mixed Applications

15. A rhombus and a square both have 4 equal sides and 2 pairs of parallel sides. How do a rhombus and a square differ?

A rhombus has n right angles.

16. In a 400-meter relay race, each runner ran one part. Their running times were 9.96 sec, 9.87 sec, 9.65 sec, and 8.97 sec. What was the team's total race time?

_38.45_

Problem-Solving Strategy

Act It Out

Brian's class is creating a bulletin board display. Each
rectangular panel is made up of hexagons, triangles,
or squares.

1. Create a rectangle using triangles
   and hexagons.

2. Create a rectangle using triangles
   and squares.

3. Create a rectangle using only
   triangles.

Mixed Applications

Solve.

┌─────── **CHOOSE A STRATEGY** ───────┐

• **Act It Out**   • **Guess and Check**   • **Work Backward**   • **Write a Number Sentence**

4. The sum of two numbers is 48.
   One of the numbers is 3 times
   the other number. What are the
   two numbers?

5. Maria bought 3 CDs at $11.99
   each. How much change did
   she get back from $40.00?

6. Charlie, Chris, Sophie, and
   Anna collected money for a
   drive. They collected a total of
   $36. If they each had raised the
   same amount, what would each
   person's share be?

7. In the classroom, there are 12
   windows on each of 2 walls.
   There are 4 windows on each of
   the other 2 walls. What is the
   total number of windows?

Name _____

Finding Perimeter

Vocabulary

Fill in the blank to complete the sentence.

1. __perimeter__ is the distance around a figure.

Find the perimeter.

2.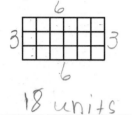

___18 units___

3.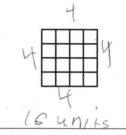

___16 units___

4.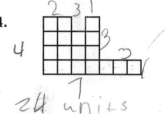

___24 units___

5.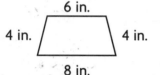

6 in.
4 in.   4 in.
8 in.

___22 units___

6.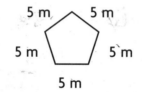

5 m   5 m
5 m   5 m
5 m

___25 m___

7.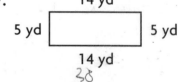

14 yd
5 yd   5 yd
14 yd
28

___38 yd___

8. 8 ft
8 ft   8 ft
8 ft

___32 ft___

9.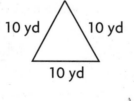

10 yd   10 yd
10 yd

___30 yd___

16
+12
28

10.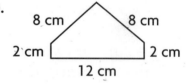

8 cm   8 cm
2 cm   2 cm
12 cm

___32 cm___

Mixed Applications

11. For a 4-mile race, 2 laps around Great Square Park are required. The park is a perfect square. What is the length of each side?

___½ mile___

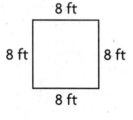

16
16
32

12. Hayes swam for 3 hours and 25 minutes. He stopped at 5:15. What time did he begin to swim?

1:50

4
8:15
3:25
1:50

:50

Exploring Area

Vocabulary

Fill in the blank to complete the sentence.

1. __Area__ is the number of square units needed to cover a flat surface.

Find the area.

2.

___7 sq units___

3.

___6 sq units___

4.

___8 sq units___

5.

___8 sq units___

6.

___8 sq units___

7.

___14 sq units___

8.

___9 sq units___

9.

___6 sq units___

10. Which figures below have the same area? __a.c.__

a.

b.

c.

d.

Mixed Applications

11. A painting in the Museum of Fine Arts is 25 feet wide and 9 feet tall. What is the area of the painting?

    ___225 sq ft.___

12. Mrs. Scopa is buying carpet for part of her classroom. She needs 6 square yards. The carpet costs $5 a square yard. How much will her carpet cost?

    ___$30.00___

Area of Irregular Figures

Find the area.

1.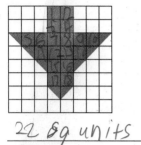

22 sq units

2.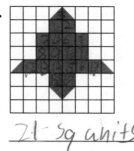

21 sq units

3.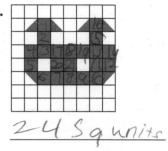

24 sq units

Estimate the area.

4.

~ 24 sq units

5.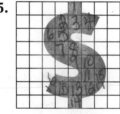

~22 sq units

6.

~ 14 sq units

Mixed Applications

7. Mark bought 10 boxes of grass seed. Each box could cover 3,000 square feet of yard. Use this drawing of Mark's house and yard to find how many boxes of grass seed Mark needs. How many boxes of seed should Mark return to the store?

9 boxes

House		

☐ = 1,000 square feet

8. Ben earned $4 an hour raking leaves. He worked 12 hours a week for 3 weeks. How much did he earn?

$144

9. George rented a video for 5 days. The first day cost $3.00. Each additional day cost $2.25. What was the cost of renting the video?

$12.00

Finding Area

Find the area.

1.
9 cm
4 cm

36 sq cm

2.
3 ft
7 ft

21 sq ft

3.
5 in.
5 in.

35 sq in

4.
4 km
8 km

32 sq km

5.
6 yd
3 yd

18 sq yd

6.
6 ft
5 ft

30 sq ft

Write the letter of the rectangle that has the greater area.

7. a.
6 cm
36 6 cm

b.
7 cm
35 5 cm

a

8. a.
8 ft
32 4 ft

b.
6 ft
30 5 ft

a

9. a.
9 yd
45 5 yd

b.
7 yd
49 7 yd

b

10. a.
6 in.
18 3 in.

b.
4 in.
16 4 in.

a

35
19
49

25
6
31

28
18
18
+18
54

Mixed Applications

11. The Claptons are buying carpet for Cindy's room and a hallway. Her bedroom is 10 feet long and 15 feet wide. The hallway is 18 feet long and 3 feet wide. How much carpet do they need?

204 sq ft.

12. Glenda is planning a 6-day trip to Quebec with her school's French club. The cost is $55 per day for hotel and food and $269 for airfare. How much will she need to pay for the trip?

$599

Relating Area and Perimeter

Write the area and the perimeter.

1.

2.

3.

9 sq units area   25 sq units area   18 sq units area

20 perimeter units   28 perimeter units   30 perimeter units

For each figure, draw another figure that has the same area but a different perimeter. Write the area in square units.

4.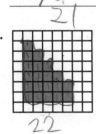

5.

6.

20 sq units   32 sq units   17 sq units

7. Which of the four figures below have the same *area* but different *perimeters*?

a, b
21

8. Which of the four figures below have the same *perimeter* but different *areas*?

b, c
14

a.

22

b.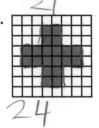

24

c.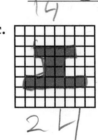

24

d.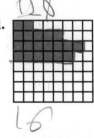

16

Mixed Applications

9. Julie's room is 10 feet long and 12 feet wide. What is the area of the floor? What is the perimeter?

120 sq feet

44 feet

10. Tobey buys two large plants for $9.98 each and a watering can for $15.00. How much does he spend?

$34.96

Problem-Solving Strategy

Draw a Diagram

Draw a diagram to solve.

1. Fiona has 20 feet of fencing to put around a garden. What is the greatest area for the garden that she can make?

   _25 sq ft._

2. Bert, Amy, Delia, and Sophia are in line to get their lunches. Bert is behind Sophia. Sophia is behind Amy. Delia is last in line. Who is third in line?

   Bert

3. Kathryn has 32 feet of fencing to put around a flower bed. What is the greatest possible area that Kathryn can make her flower bed?

   _64 sq ft_

4. Nadeem has 16 feet of fencing to make a pen for his dog. What shape will provide the greatest area? What will be the lengths of the sides?

   Square 4ft × 4ft

Mixed Applications

Solve.

CHOOSE A STRATEGY

- Act It Out
- Make an Organized List
- Work Backward

5. On the lunch menu are tuna, chicken, pasta, and garden salads. Each salad comes in medium or large size. How many lunch choices are there?

   8 choices

6. Emma wants to make 6 scarecrows to stop birds from eating her corn. She needs 4 pieces of wood for each scarecrow. How many pieces of wood does she need?

   24 pieces of wood

7. Jane spent half her money at the grocery store. Then she spent half of what was left at the tape store. She had $11 when she got home. How much money did she have to start?

   _$44.00_

Translations, Reflections, and Rotations

Vocabulary

Write the letter of the phrase that best describes each word.

1. __C__ reflection

2. __A__ translation

3. __D__ transformation

4. __B__ rotation

A. when you slide a figure

B. when you turn a figure around a point or a vertex

C. when you flip a figure over a line

D. when you move a figure

Copy each figure on dot paper. Draw figures to show a *translation*, *reflection*, and *rotation* for each.

5. Original   Translation   Reflection   Rotation

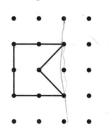  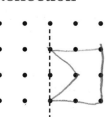 

6. Original   Translation   Reflection   Rotation

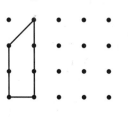 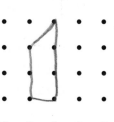 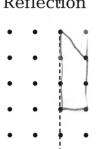 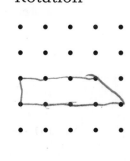

Mixed Applications

7. Eraldo walks past the gym on one side of Walnut Street. How many turns must she make to be walking in the opposite direction on the other side of Walnut Street?

   __2 turns__

8. Anna has 84 equal-sized photographs to put in her album. Each page of the album holds 6 photographs. How many pages will Anna's photographs take up?

   __14 pages__

Name _____

Congruence

Vocabulary

Fill in the blanks.

1. ___congruent figures___ have the same size and shape.

Trace one figure in each pair. Place it over the second figure to check for congruency. Write whether each pair is congruent.

2.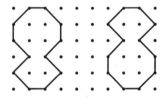

Congruent

3.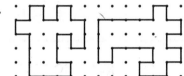

Not congruent

4. 21   21

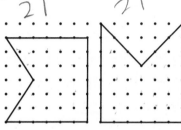

Congruent

Is each pair of figures congruent? Write *yes* or *no*.

5.

yes

6.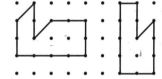

_no_

7.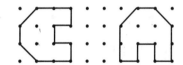

yes

Mixed Applications

8. Sophia and Emma both have rectangular rooms that have the same perimeter. Are their rooms congruent? Explain.

_____

_____

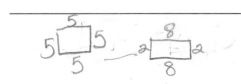

9. A school raised money to save rain-forest land. The money was used to buy 9 acres at $35 an acre. How much money was raised?

$3.15

35 35 35 35

35
× 9

$315

Two Kinds of Symmetry

Vocabulary

Fill in the blanks.

1. A figure has ___paint___ ___symmety___ if it can be turned about a central point, and still look the same in at least two different positions.

On a separate sheet of paper, trace each figure and cut it out. Label the corners of the traced figure with numbers. Turn the traced figure about its central point to determine whether it has point symmetry. Write *yes* or *no*.

2.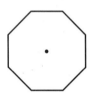

___y15___

3.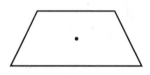

___ng___

4.

___yes___

5.

___yes___

6.

___yes___

7.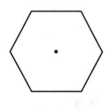

___yes___

Mixed Applications

8. Jonathan is measuring the perimeter of the playground. What is the perimeter of the playground if it is a rhombus?

108 ft

___432ft___

9. Boston University has 15,568 undergraduate students. Boston College has 8,896. How many more students attend Boston University than Boston College?

___6,672___

More About Symmetry

Vocabulary

Fill in the blanks.

1. A figure has ___line___ ___symmetry___ when it can be folded about a line so that its two parts are identical.

Complete the design to show line symmetry.

2.
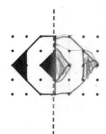

3.
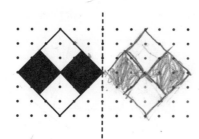

4.

Draw the other half of the figure to show that it has line symmetry.

5.
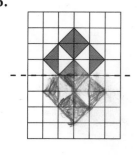

6.
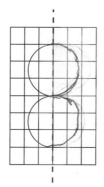

7.
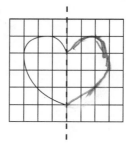

8.
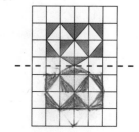

Mixed Applications

9. Name 3 things in your classroom that have line symmetry.

_____

10. Curtis spent half his money on a concert ticket. He spent half his remaining money on a T-shirt. He had $16 left over. How much did Curtis begin with?

$64

_____

Tessellations

Vocabulary

Fill in the blank.

1. When you arrange polygons to cover a surface without leaving any space between them or making them overlap,

   you are making a ___Tessellation___.

Will the polygon tessellate? Use tracings of the polygon to help you decide. Write *yes* or *no*.

2.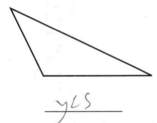

   ___yes___

3.

   ___yes___

4.

   ___no___

Write the names of the polygons that tessellate in each design.

5.

   ___rhombus___

6.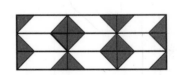

   ___triangle___
   ___parallelogram___

7.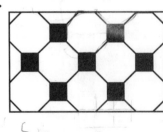

   ___square___
   ___octagon___

Mixed Applications

8. Draw your own tessellating pattern. Use two different shapes.

9. How many 6-inch square tiles would you need to cover the floor of a bathroom that is 4 feet wide by 5 feet long?

   _____

Name Emily Ann Kigh-

Changing Sizes of Shapes

Vocabulary

Fill in the blank.

1. When you enlarge or reduce a figure, it is _Simillari_
   to the original figure. The two figures have the same shape
   but not the same size.

Enlarge each figure by using the grid below.

2.

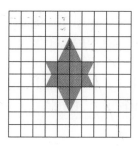

3.

4.

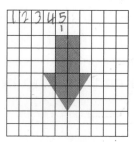

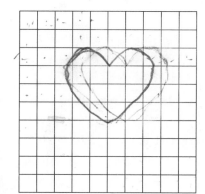

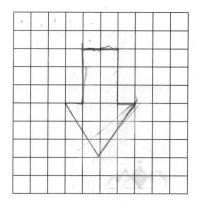

Mixed Applications

5. Peter has a one-page map of
   the United States in his history
   book. There is also a United
   States wall map in his classroom. Are the maps similar?
   Explain.

6. Brian works for 3 hours and
   takes a 15-minute break. Then
   he works for 2 hours and 30
   minutes before quitting at
   3:15 P.M. What time did Brian
   begin work?

9:30 A.m

Problem-Solving Strategy

Make a Model

Make a model to solve.

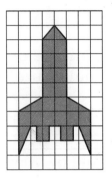

1. Suppose you want to make a larger picture of the figure at the right to put on a poster. Use one-inch grid paper, and copy the figure, square by square, to make a larger picture.

2. Aber has 36 feet of fencing to make a pen for her ferret. What is the greatest possible area she can enclose with her fence?

   81 Sqare ft.

3. Billy's house has 6 windows on the front wall and 6 on the back wall. There are 3 windows on each side wall. What is the total number of windows on Billy's house?

   18 windows

Mixed Applications

Solve.

| CHOOSE A STRATEGY |
| • Act It out • Use a Table • Make an Organized List • Write a Number Sentence |

4. Pieter spent half his money on a movie ticket, and half his remaining money on snacks. He has $4 remaining. How much money did Pieter begin with?

   $16.00

5. Four students stand in line. Alex is after Ben and before Mindy. Colby is after Ben and before Alex. If Alex is next to Mindy, in what order are the students?

   Ben, colby, Alex, mindy

6. Marcia went to a florist to buy a dozen identical roses. She paid $30.00 for the dozen. About how much did each rose cost?

   b Ctweten$2 andB

7. The school chorus has 39 students. There are twice as many boys as girls. How many boys are in the chorus?

   26 boys

Name _____

Multiplying by Multiples

Vocabulary

Complete.

1. A __multiple__ is the product of a given number and another whole number.

Finish each pattern.

2. $3 \times \underline{20} = 60$

$\underline{3} \times 200 = 600$

$3 \times 2,000 = \underline{6,000}$

3. $\underline{6} \times 30 = 180$

$6 \times 300 = \underline{1800}$

$6 \times \underline{3,000} = 18,000$

4. $5 \times 40 = \underline{200}$

$5 \times \underline{400} = 2,000$

$\underline{5} \times 4,000 = 20,000$

5. $4 \times 40 = \underline{160}$

$4 \times \underline{400} = 1,600$

$\underline{4} \times 4,000 = 16,000$

6. $2 \times 50 = \underline{100}$

$\underline{2} \times 500 = 1,000$

$2 \times \underline{5,000} = 10,000$

7. $7 \times \underline{60} = 420$

$7 \times 600 = \underline{4200}$

$\underline{7} \times 6,000 = 42,000$

Use mental math and basic multiplication facts to find the product.

8. $6 \times 20 = \underline{120}$

9. $5 \times 300 = \underline{1,500}$

10. $4 \times 1,000 = \underline{4,000}$

11. $4 \times 5,000 = \underline{20,000}$

12. $8 \times 400 = \underline{3200}$

13. $9 \times 30 = \underline{270}$

14. $\begin{array}{r} 70 \\ \times\ 5 \\ \hline 350 \end{array}$

15. $\begin{array}{r} 500 \\ \times\ 8 \\ \hline 4,000 \end{array}$

16. $\begin{array}{r} 4,000 \\ \times\ 7 \\ \hline 28,000 \end{array}$

17. $\begin{array}{r} 600 \\ \times\ 9 \\ \hline 5400 \end{array}$

Mixed Applications

18. A local charity donated $400 to each of 7 schools. What was the charity's total donation?

$2,800

19. Marcia's room is 10 feet long and 12 feet wide. What is the area of Marcia's room?

126 sq. ft.

A Way to Multiply

Use base-ten blocks. Find the product.

1. Vinny's Gym ordered 8 barbells. Each barbell weighed 45 pounds. How much did the 8 barbells weigh in all?

_360 lb_

2. Patricia bought 6 framed posters. Each poster cost $50. How much did the 6 posters cost in all?

_$300_

3. Each of the 24 students in Ms. Khalsa's class brought in 7 cans to recycle. How many cans did Ms. Khalsa's students recycle?

168 cans

4. A dentist received 6 boxes of toothbrushes. Each box contained 60 toothbrushes. How many toothbrushes did the dentist receive in all?

360 toothbrush

5. Bill's local high school has 7 class periods each day. Each class period is 45 minutes. How many class minutes are there each day?

315 min.

6. Jean-Claude bought 5 apples at a supermarket. Each apple cost $0.69. How much did the 5 apples cost?

_$3.45_

7. $\begin{array}{r} 21 \\ \times\ 9 \\ \hline 189 \end{array}$

8. $\begin{array}{r} \overset{3}{49} \\ \times\ 4 \\ \hline 196 \end{array}$

9. $\begin{array}{r} \overset{2}{38} \\ \times\ 3 \\ \hline 114 \end{array}$

10. $\begin{array}{r} 51 \\ \times\ 7 \\ \hline 357 \end{array}$

11. $\begin{array}{r} \overset{1}{42} \\ \times\ 6 \\ \hline 252 \end{array}$

Mixed Applications

12. Mr. Chavez paid $43 to each student who helped with his sculpture. There were 6 students who helped. What was the total amount that Mr. Chavez paid the students?

_$258_

13. Anna has 40 feet of fencing for a rabbit cage. What is the greatest possible area that she can make her rabbit cage?

_100_

Modeling Multiplication

Vocabulary

Fill in the blank.

1. When the ones and tens are multiplied separately,

   each product is called a _Partial proudct_.

```
    32 ──── Factors
  ×  4
  ─────
     8 ──── Partial
 +120       Products
 ─────
   128 ──── Final
            Product
```

Use place-value mats and base-ten blocks to find the product.

2. 18
    × 6
    ───
    108

3. 29
    × 4
    ───
    116

4. 53
    × 5
    ───
    115

5. 74
    × 3
    ───
    222

6. 36
    × 8
    ───
    288

7. 44
    × 7
    ───
    308

8. 64
    × 5
    ───
    320

9. 87
    × 2
    ───
    174

Find each product by using partial products.

10. 33
     × 6
     ───
     198

11. 41
     × 5
     ───
     205

12. 46
     × 7
     ───
     304

13. 28
     × 8
     ───
     206

14. 78
     × 3
     ───
     238

15. 57
     × 2
     ───
     164

16. 61
     × 4
     ───
     244

17. 38
     × 9
     ───
     297

Mixed Applications

18. Alexander used 6 rolls of film during a family trip. He took 36 pictures with each roll of film. How many pictures did Alexander take?

    _____

19. Tyrone spent half his money on CDs. He then spent half his remaining money on books. Tyrone has $18 left. How much money did Tyrone have to begin with?

    $72.00

Recording Multiplication

Multiply. Tell in which place-value positions you need to regroup.

1. 174 _____
   × 4
   796

2. 261 _____
   × 3
   783

3. 432 _____
   × 5
   2160

4. 364 _____
   × 2
   728

5. 512 _____
   × 6
   3072

6. 134 _____
   × 7
   938

Find the product.

7. 236
   × 4
   944

8. 387
   × 6
   2342

9. 631
   × 4
   2524

10. 136
    × 8
    1088

11. 226
    × 5
    1130

12. 308
    × 3
    924

13. 426
    × 7
    2982

14. 913
    × 4
    3652

Mixed Applications

15. In Mr. Wilson's class, 8 students each read a 612-page book on pioneers. What was the total number of pages read?

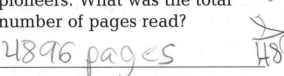

4896 pages

16. Madeleine chose balloons for the school party. She could choose among red, green, and blue balloons. She could also choose among small, medium, and large balloons. List the different balloons Madeleine could buy.

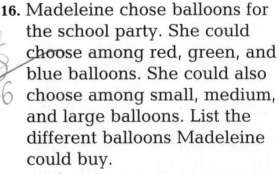

rs, rm, rl, gs, gm gl, bs, bm, bl.

17. Among the cats registered in the United States, 47,022 are Persian cats and 3,852 are Maine Coon cats. How many more Persian cats are registered?

43,270

Practicing Multiplication

Multiply, and record each product. Place the dollar sign and
decimal point in it.

1. $3.99
    × 6
    $23.94

2. $4.01
    × 5
    20.05

3. $2.79
    × 4
    $11.16

4. $1.75
    × 8
    $14.00

5. $2.66
    × 9
    $23.94

6. $0.59
    × 7
    $4.13

7. $5.88
    × 3
    $17.64

8. $7.31
    × 5
    $36.55

9. $9.99
    × 6
    $59.94

10. $6.55
    × 3
    $19.65

11. $2.65
    × 8
    $21.20

12. $6.46
    × 4
    $25.84

    2.46
    × 7
    $17.22

13. $6.05
    × 9
    54.45

14. $4.33
    × 7
    $30.31

15. $5.25
    × 6
    $31.50

16. $1.89
    × 5
    $9.54

17. 3 × $1.45 = $4.35

18. 7 × $2.46 = $17.22

Mixed Applications

For Problems 19 and 20, use the price list.

PRICE LIST	
Pencils (box of 10)	$1.49
Erasers (3 per set)	$0.79
Paper (12 pads per package)	$4.99

19. David bought 2 boxes of pencils
    and 1 set of erasers for school.
    How much did David spend?

    $3.77

20. Katrina bought 1 package of
    paper, 2 sets of erasers, and
    1 box of pencils. How much did
    the items she bought cost?

    $8.06

21. Mrs. O'Connell is training for a
    long-distance bicycle race. She
    rides 36 miles each morning
    and 72 miles each afternoon.
    How many miles does she ride
    in 5 days?

    540miles

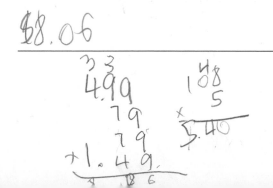
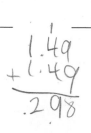

Problem-Solving Strategy

Write a Number Sentence

Write a number sentence to solve the problem.

1. Lucy bought 7 CDs that cost $11.99 each. How much did she spend for the 7 CDs?

$7 \times \$11.99 = n$

$n = \$83.93$

2. Amanda wants to take swimming lessons at the YMCA. The lessons cost $49.95 each month. How much money will she need for 8 months of lessons?

$\$49.95 \times 8 = n, n = \$399.60$

3. Nelson runs the 26-mile marathon at a pace of 7 minutes per mile. How many minutes does it take Nelson to complete the marathon?

$26 \times 7 = n, n = 182 \text{ min.}$

4. Two local schools collected food for a homeless shelter. Sage School collected 3,145 pounds of food. Charles River School collected 169 fewer pounds of food. How many pounds of food did Charles River collect?

$3,145 - 169 = n$

$n = 2,976 \text{ lb}$

Mixed Applications

Solve.

┌─ CHOOSE A STRATEGY ─┐

• Write a Number Sentence   • Make an Organized List   • Act It Out   • Make a Model

5. Five students stood in a line. Barbara was in the middle. Beverly stood next to Barbara. Mark was at the right end. Ben stood between Barbara and Mark. Where was Andy?

Left end

6. A basketball team sells team jerseys, T-shirts, and sweatshirts. All are available in purple or gold. List the different shirt combinations sold.

gj, pj, gT, pT, gs, ps,

Patterns with Multiples

Complete. Use a basic fact and the pattern of zeros to help you.

1. $4 \times 30 = $ 120

  $4 \times 300 = $ 1,200

  $4 \times 3,000 = $ 12,000

2. $5 \times 70 = $ 350

  $50 \times 70 = $ 3,500

  $50 \times 700 = $ 350,000

3. $6 \times 40 = $ 240

  $60 \times 40 = $ 2,400

  $60 \times 400 = $ 24,000

4. $20 \times 80 = $ 1,600

  $20 \times 800 = $ 16,000

  $20 \times 8,000 = $ 160,000

5. $7 \times 60 = $ 420

  $70 \times 600 = $ 42,000

  $70 \times 6,000 = $ 420,000

6. $3 \times 50 = $ 150

  $30 \times 500 = $ 15,000

  $30 \times 5,000 = $ 150,000

Use mental math and basic facts to find the product.

7. $4 \times 40 = $ 160

8. $80 \times 30 = $ 2400

9. $5 \times 900 = $ 4,500

10. $70 \times 400 = $ 28,000

11. $3 \times 7,000 = $ 21,000

12. $50 \times 200 = $ 10,000

Find the product.

13. $\begin{array}{r} 80 \\ \times\ 4 \\ \hline 320 \end{array}$

14. $\begin{array}{r} 90 \\ \times 60 \\ \hline 5400 \end{array}$

15. $\begin{array}{r} 700 \\ \times\ 7 \\ \hline 4900 \end{array}$

16. $\begin{array}{r} 600 \\ \times\ 50 \\ \hline 30000 \end{array}$

Mixed Applications

17. A chain of 30 record stores sold a new CD. Each store sold out of its supply of 500 CDs. How many of this new CD were sold by the record-store chain?

  15,000 CDs

18. The school cafeteria received eight 40-lb boxes of pasta. If the carrying cart can hold no more than 150 lb, how many trips will be needed to move the boxes?

  3 trips

Problem-Solving Strategy

Find a Pattern

Find a pattern and solve.

1. A school yearbook had 20 student pictures on every other page starting with page 1. It was 40 pages long. How many student pictures did the yearbook contain?

   400 pictures

2. Laurie has a puzzle for her classmates. When she says 17, the answer is 12. When she says 40, the answer is 35. When she says 51, the answer is 46. What is the pattern?

   _−5_

3. Football players on a college team weigh an average of 200 pounds. If there are 60 players on the team, about how much is the total weight of the team?

   12,000 pounds

4. Oscar scores about 80 points on each quiz. If he takes 30 quizzes, about how many total points will he score?

   2,400 points

Mixed Applications

Solve.

┌─── **CHOOSE A STRATEGY** ───┐

• **Write a Number Sentence**   • **Act It Out**   • **Make a Model**   • **Find a Pattern**

5. Helena earned $6 per hour for the first 20 hours per week she worked. She earned $9 per hour for any additional hours. If Helena worked 27 hours in a week, how much did she earn?

   _$183_

6. Monica's room is 12 feet wide and 9 feet long. What is the total area of Monica's room? What is the perimeter?

   _108 sf._

   _42 ft_

7. Conrad bought an energy bar for $1.25 and a pencil for $0.65. He paid with a $5 bill. How much change did he get back?

   _3.10_

8. Morgan is making a rectangular rabbit pen that is 8 feet long and 4 feet wide. In yards, what is the perimeter of the pen?

   _8 yd_

Estimating Products with Multiples

Round each factor to the nearest ten. Estimate the product.

1. 27 _30_
   ×14 _10_
   _300_

2. 54 _50_
   ×46 _50_
   _2500_

3. 36 _40_
   ×17 _20_
   _800_

4. 84 _80_
   ×19 _20_
   _1600_

5. 63 _60_ 6 12
   ×27 _30_ 0
   × _____
   _1800_

6. 44 _40_
   ×31 _30_
   _1200_

7. 75 _70_
   ×24 _20_
   _1400_

8. 46 _50_
   ×15 _20_
   _1000_

9. 95 _100_
   ×46 _50_
   _5000_

10. 38 _40_
    ×42 _40_
    _1600_

44
4
4

Round each factor. Estimate the product.

11. $25 _30_
    × 16 _20_
    _600_

12. 54 _50_
    ×27 _30_
    _1500_

13. $451 _500_
    × 36 _40_
    _20,000_

14. 742 _700_
    × 45 _50_
    _35,000_

4
4

15. 23 × 76 = _1,600_   _20_ _80_

16. 18 × 74 = _1,400_   _20_ _70_

17. 56 × 322 = _18,000_   _60_ _300_

18. 51 × 437 = _20,000_   _50_ _400_

19. 35 × 525 = _20,000_   _40_ _500_

20. 72 × 727 = _49,000_   _70_ _700_

21. 68 × 494 = _35,000_   _70_ _500_

22. 44 × 863 = _36,000_   _40_ _900_

Mixed Applications

23. The average class size at one school is 25. There are 17 classes in the school. Estimate the total number of students.

    _30_
    _20_
    × _____
    _600_

    600 Students

24. Marge spent $4 for a magazine. She spent half of her remaining money on a T-shirt. Then she spent $2 on a snack. Marge had $14 remaining. How much money did Marge begin with?

    _20_
    _30_
    × _____
    _600_

    _$36_

25. Dan is 4 inches taller than Mike. Together they are 8 feet 8 inches tall. How tall, in feet and inches, is each boy?

    D4ft 6inch, M 4ft 2inches

26. There are 30 rows of chairs in the auditorium. There are 20 students in each row and 9 students on the stage. How many students are in the auditorium?

    609 students

Modeling Multiplication

Use the model to write a number sentence and find the product.

1.

```
 100
  40
  70
+ 28
-----
 238
```

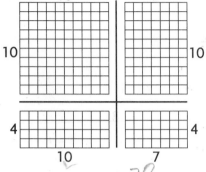

$$14 \times 17 = 238$$

2.

```
200
 40
120
 24
+
---
384
```

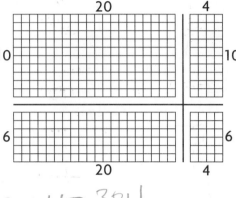 

$$16 \times 24 = 384$$

Find the product. You may wish to make a model.

3.
```
   14
 ×12
 ----
   28
+140
 ----
  168
```

4.
```
   18
 ×11
 ----
   18
  180
 ----
  198
```

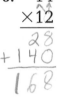

5.
```
   23
 ×15
 ----
  115
+230
 ----
  345
```

6.
```
    5
   19
 ×16
 ----
  114
  190
 ----
  304
```

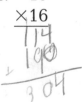

7.
```
    2
   27
 ×14
 ----
  108
+270
 ----
  378
```

8.
```
    1
   25
 ×13
 ----
   75
  250
 ----
  325
```

```
23
×5
---
115

23
10
---
230
```

Mixed Applications

9. A mail-order catalogue receives about 900 orders in a day. If the average order is about $60, what is the value of one day's worth of orders?

$54,000

10. Brian has more trading cards than Ben. Alex has more trading cards than Meghan. Alex has 19 fewer cards than Ben. Who has the most trading cards?

Brian

Name _____

Recording Multiplication

Find the product.

1.
```
    62
  × 35
  1310
+ 1860
  2,170
```

2.
```
    55
  × 29
   495
+ 1100
  1,595
```

3.
```
    73
  × 44
   292
+ 2920
  3,212
```

4.
```
    48
  × 27
   336
+ 960
  1,290
```

5.
```
    81
  × 17
   567
+ 810
  1,377
```

6.
```
    67
  × 23
   201
+ 1340
  1,541
```

7.
```
    26
  × 18
   208
+ 260
   468
```

8.
```
    32
  × 24
   128
+ 640
   768
```

9.
```
  $74
  × 16
  444
  740
+
  1,184
```

10.
```
    69
  × 36
   414
  2070
+
  2,484
```

11.
```
   $39
  × 35
   195
+ 1170
  1,365
```

12.
```
    76
  × 11
   176
   760
+
   836
```

13.
```
   $87
  × 37
   609
+ 2610
  3,219
```

14.
```
    52
  × 29
   468
+ 1,040
  1,508
```

15.
```
    41
  × 22
   182
+ 820
   902
```

16.
```
   $94
  × 49
   846
+ 3,760
  4,606
```

17. $14 \times 53 =$ ___742___

18. $\$26 \times 77 =$ ___2,002___

19. $38 \times 41 =$ ___1,558___

20. $49 \times 86 =$ ___4,214___

21. $\$26 \times 74 =$ ___$1924___

22. $21 \times 79 =$ ___1,659___

Mixed Applications

23. Derek measured the outside of his house. The length is 37 feet and the width is 40 feet. What is the area of Derek's house?

___1,480 sqft___

24. What time of day is it when the hour hand is perpendicular to the minute hand and the minute hand points to the number 12?

___3:00 or 9:00___

Practicing Multiplication

Find the product.

1. 221
    × 17
    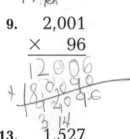
    1547
    +2210
    3757

2. $447
    × 36
    2682
    +13,410
    16,092

3. 727
    × 32
    1454
    +21810
    +2,3264

4. 362
    × 27
    2534
    +1240
    3774

5. 549
    × 22
    1098
    +10080
    12078

6. $7.29
    × 46
    4374
    +29160
    33534

7. 636
    × 34
    2948
    +10180
    22128
    133

8. 659
    × 73
    1977
    +43430
    5,404

9. 2,001
    × 96
    12006
    +18,0090
    3 14

10. $2,425
    × 24
    9700
    +49500
    60200

11. 3,478
    × 47
    24256
    +139120
    163376
    244

12. $56.99
    × 26
    33834
    +113980
    147874

13. 1,527
    × 76
    19,162
    +106890
    116052

14. 3,639
    × 69
    32751
    +203340
    2.36091

15. 7,498
    × 55
    37490
    374900
    412390

16. 6,643
    × 78
    33144
    525010
    55 8,154

17. 74 × 138 = _____

18. 25 × 808 = _____

19. 89 × $465 = _____

20. 19 × $51.75 = _____

21. 48 × 2,769 = _____

22. 36 × 4,873 = _____

Mixed Applications

23. A bookstore sold 78 paperbacks priced at $3.99 each and 34 hardcover books priced at $24.99 each. What was the total amount of sales for paperback and hardcover books?

_____

24. An ordinary shower head sprays 4 gallons of water per minute. If one person takes a 5-minute shower, how many gallons of water will be used?

_____

Name _____

Modeling Division

Use base-ten blocks to model and record each problem.

1. Jane picked 34 flowers. If she divides the flowers evenly in 2 vases, how many flowers can she put in each vase?

17 flower

2. A package of balloons contains an equal number of red, white, and blue balloons. If there are 45 balloons in all, how many balloons of each color are there?

15 balloons

Make a model and solve.

3. $51 \div 3 =$ _17_   4. $68 \div 4 =$ _17_   5. $65 \div 5 =$ _13_   6. $91 \div 7 =$ _13_

7. $63 \div 3 =$ _21_   8. $76 \div 4 =$ _19_   9. $96 \div 6 =$ _16_   10. $58 \div 2 =$ _29_

11. $38 \div 2 =$ _19_   12. $52 \div 4 =$ _13_   13. $48 \div 3 =$ _16_   14. $72 \div 6 =$ _12_

Mixed Applications

For Problems 15–19, use the table. The students in Mr. Jackson's class are holding a bake sale.

15. If Sara divides the chocolate chip cookies evenly into 3 bags, how many cookies does she put into each bag?

14 cookies

Kind of Cookie	Total Number
Chocolate chip	42
Oatmeal	65
Ginger	48

16. If Tim divides the oatmeal cookies evenly into 5 bags, how many cookies does he put into each bag?

13 cookies

17. How many ginger cookies can Steve put into each bag if he uses 3 bags?

16 cookies

18. Mrs. Davis bought 2 bags of cookies for $1.75 per bag. How much did she spend in all?

_$3.50_

19. Mr. Brown bought one bag of cookies for $1.75. What was his change from a $10 bill?

_$8.25_

Dividing with Remainders

Vocabulary

1. In a division problem, the __remainder__ is the amount left over when a number is not evenly divided.

Find the quotient.

2.
$$\begin{array}{r} 4\ r3 \\ 4\overline{)19} \\ -16 \\ \hline 3 \end{array}$$

3.
$$\begin{array}{r} 8\ r1 \\ 3\overline{)25} \\ -24 \\ \hline 1 \end{array}$$

4.
$$\begin{array}{r} 6\ r2 \\ 6\overline{)38} \\ -36 \\ \hline 2 \end{array}$$

5.
$$\begin{array}{r} 8\ r1 \\ 2\overline{)17} \\ 16 \\ \hline 1 \end{array}$$

6.
$$\begin{array}{r} 8\ r15 \\ 7\overline{)61} \\ -56 \\ \hline 15 \end{array}$$

7.
$$\begin{array}{r} 9\ r2 \\ 5\overline{)47} \\ -45 \\ \hline 2 \end{array}$$

8.
$$\begin{array}{r} 6\ r1 \\ 3\overline{)19} \\ 18 \\ \hline 1 \end{array}$$

9.
$$\begin{array}{r} 5\ r3 \\ 8\overline{)43} \\ 40 \\ \hline 3 \end{array}$$

Mixed Applications

10. A school auditorium has 14 rows of seats, with 20 seats in each row. If there are 200 people sitting in the auditorium, how many seats are empty?

    ___80 seats___

11. If 5 boys divide a set of marbles evenly, would there ever be more than 4 marbles left over? Explain.

    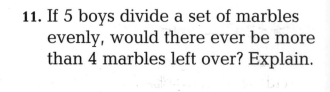

12. Jane deals out the same number of playing cards to 6 players. If there are 52 cards in all, how many cards are left over?

    ___4 cards___

13. George's father is 4 times as old as George. George is 2 years older than his brother Tim. George's father is 36. How old is Tim?

    7

Division Procedures

Find the quotient. Check by multiplying.

1. 2)64   Check:

2. 3)96   Check:

3. 4)51   Check:

4. 3)94   Check:

5. 7)93   Check:

6. 8)89   Check:

Mixed Applications

7. A piece of paper is 9 inches wide and 12 inches long. What is the area of the paper? What is the perimeter?

   108 sq.in. 42 in.

8. A football stadium can seat 50,000 people. If 25,000 seats are empty, how many people are attending the game?

   25,000 peoples

9. Bill has 98 pencils. Can he divide them evenly into 4 boxes? Explain.

   no

10. Carrie left school at 2:40. It took her 15 minutes to get home. She spent 10 minutes having a snack. How many minutes does she have left before soccer practice at 4:00?

    55 min.

Placing the First Digit in the Quotient

Put an **x** where the first digit in the quotient should be placed.

1. $5\overline{)36}$ 7 r1

2. $3\overline{)62}$ 20 r2

3. $2\overline{)173}$ 86 r1

4. $6\overline{)72}$ 12

5. $4\overline{)241}$ 60 r1

6. $7\overline{)702}$ 100 r2

7. $9\overline{)381}$ 42 r3

8. $4\overline{)820}$ 205

Find the quotient. Check by multiplying.

9. $6\overline{)45}$ Check: 7 r3

10. $3\overline{)84}$ Check: 28

11. $5\overline{)149}$ Check: 29 r4

12. $2\overline{)157}$ Check: 78 r1

13. $3\overline{)171}$ Check: 57

14. $7\overline{)823}$ Check: 117 r4

Mixed Applications

15. The school bus can seat 76 students. Each row seats 4 students. How many rows of seats are there in the bus?

    19 rows

16. A farmer has 12 cows and 32 chickens. How many animal legs are there?

    112 legs

Problem-Solving Strategy

Guess and Check

Use guess and check and solve.

1. There were 93 students going to a nature camp. After equal groups were formed for hiking, 2 students were left over. There were fewer than 10 students in each group. How many groups were formed?

13 groups

2. During a hike, Sally and Dave collected 160 acorns. Sally collected 3 times as many acorns as Dave. How many acorns did Dave collect?

40 acorns

3. The 93 nature camp students ate lunch at the lodge. They sat at an even number of tables. There were 5 students sitting at one table, and an equal number of students sitting at each of the other tables. How many students were sitting at each of the other tables?

8 students

4. At one table, some of the students shared 3 pizzas. Each pizza was cut into 8 slices. After the students shared the pizza equally, there were 3 slices left over. How many students shared the pizza? How many slices of pizza did each student eat?

7 students
3 slices

Mixed Applications

Solve.

┌──── CHOOSE A STRATEGY ────┐

• **Guess and Check**   • **Write a Number Sentence**   • **Find a Pattern**   • **Make a Table**

5. Dave was organizing his collection of 137 seeds. When he put the same number of seeds into each box, he had 2 seeds left over. There were either 4, 5, or 6 seeds in each box. How many boxes did Dave use?

27 boxes

6. Carol put 37 flowers into vases. She put 4 flowers into each green vase, and 3 flowers into each white vase. How many green and white vases might she have used?

4 green
7 white

Dividing Three-Digit Numbers

Put an **x** where the first digit in the quotient should be placed.

1. 4)137

2. 3)325

3. 2)198

4. 7)924

5. 6)230

6. 3)591

7. 9)290

8. 4)400

Find the quotient. Check by multiplying.

9. 3)152   Check:
   50 r 2
   -15
   02
            50
          × 3
          150
         + 2
          152

10. 2)542   Check:
    271
    -4
     14
    -14
     02
    -2
      0
            271
          - 2
          542

11. 5)627   Check:
    125 r 2
    5
    12
    -10
    27
    -25
    0
            125
          × 5
          625
          627

12. 324 ÷ 6 = __54__   Check:
                        54
                      × 6
                      324

13. 647 ÷ 9 = __71 r8__   Check:
                          71
                        × 9
                        639
                        + 8
                        647

Mixed Applications

14. There are 118 children who want to play softball. How many teams of 9 can be formed?

    __13 teams, 1 left__

15. There were 94 people watching a game. Three people were standing. An equal number of people were sitting on 13 benches. How many people were seated on each bench?

    __7 people__

Practicing Division

Find the quotient. Check by multiplying.

1. 2)745   Check:

$$372 r9$$

6
14
- 14
05
4

372
× 2
744
+ 1
745

2. 4)423   Check:

$$105 r3$$

4
023
- 20
3

105
× 4
420
+ 3
423

3. 5)135   Check:

$$27$$

10
35
- 35
0

27
× 5
135

4. 7)931   Check:

$$133$$

7
23
- 21
21

133
× 7
931

5. 3)322   Check:

$$107 r1$$

3
022
21
1

107
× 3
321
+ 1
322

6. 4)728   Check:

$$182$$

- 4
32
- 32
08
8

182
× 4
728

7. 345 ÷ 5 = __69__   Check:

69
× 5
345

8. 726 ÷ 6 = __121__   Check:

121
× 6
726

Mixed Applications

9. There are 364 stickers in a
package. If 5 children share
the stickers equally, how many
stickers will each person get?
How many stickers will be
left over?

__72 r4__

10. A snail climbs a wall that is
16 feet high. Each day the snail
climbs 5 feet, but each night it
slips back down 3 feet. How
many days will it take for the
snail to get to the top of the
wall?

__8 days__

Name _____

Division Patterns to Estimate

Complete. Use a basic fact and a pattern of zeros to help you.

1. $240 \div \underline{6} = 40$ 2. $350 \div 5 = \underline{70}$ 3. $\underline{360} \div 4 = 90$

   $2{,}400 \div 6 = \underline{400}$ $3{,}500 \div \underline{5} = 700$ $3{,}600 \div 4 = \underline{900}$

   $\underline{24{,}000} \div 6 = 4{,}000$ $\underline{35{,}000} \div 5 = 7{,}000$ $36{,}000 \div \underline{4} = 9{,}000$

Find the quotient.

4. $3\overline{)210}$ quotient 70

5. $4\overline{)2{,}800}$ quotient 700

6. $2\overline{)8{,}000}$ quotient $4{,}000$

7. $9\overline{)450}$ quotient 50

8. $7\overline{)49{,}000}$ quotient $7{,}000$

9. $8\overline{)40{,}000}$ quotient $5{,}000$

10. $8\overline{)3{,}200}$ quotient 400

11. $4\overline{)120}$ quotient 30

12. $6\overline{)36{,}000}$ quotient $6{,}000$

13. $5\overline{)2{,}000}$ quotient 400

Estimate. Use a pattern of zeros to find the quotient.

14. $4{,}512 \div 9 = n$

   $4{,}500 \div 9 = 500$

15. $423 \div 6 = n$

   $420 \div 6 = 70$

16. $32{,}123 \div 8 = n$

   $32{,}000 \div 8 = 4{,}000$

17. $281 \div 4 = n$

   $280 \div 4 = 70$

18. $5{,}419 \div 6 = n$

   $5{,}400 \div 6 = 900$

19. $15{,}120 \div 5 = n$

   $15{,}000 \div 5 = 3{,}000$

Mixed Applications

For Problems 20–22, use the table at the right.

20. The Shaw family drove from Boston to Houston in 6 days. If they drove about the same distance each day, about how many miles did they drive each day?

   $1800 \div 6 = 300$

ROAD MILEAGE FROM BOSTON, MA	
To City	**Number of Miles**
Kansas City, MO	1,391
Philadelphia, PA	296
Houston, TX	1,804

21. The Peters family drove from Boston to Philadelphia at an average speed of 50 miles per hour. About how many hours did they drive?

   $300 \div 50 = 6 \text{ hours}$

22. Tom and his family left Boston on Monday morning to drive to Kansas City. If they drove about 200 miles each day, what day did they arrive at Kansas City?

   $1400 \div 200 = 7$

     Sunday

Zeros in Division

Write the number of digits in each quotient.

1. 4)364

2. 6)612

3. 3)411

4. 7)105

5. 5)545

6. 8)432

7. 7)905

8. 2)123

Find the quotient.

9. 3)312

10. 4)429

11. 6)526

12. 4)436

13. 6)724

14. 5)531

15. 9)230

16. 7)903

Mixed Applications

17. Isaac delivers a total of 724 newspapers during the week. He delivers the same number of newspapers on each weekday, Monday through Friday. He delivers a total of 204 newspapers on Saturday and Sunday. How many newspapers does he deliver on Monday?

    104 papers

18. The *Brookfield News* prints 5,125 copies of the newspaper each weekday. How many copies are printed in 5 weekdays?

    25,625 copies

Practicing Division

Find the quotient. Place the dollar sign and decimal point in the quotient.

1. $\begin{array}{r}\$1.85 \\ 4\overline{)\$7.40}\end{array}$ 2. $\begin{array}{r}\$1.26 \\ 5\overline{)\$6.30}\end{array}$ 3. $\begin{array}{r}\$1.38 \\ 6\overline{)\$8.28}\end{array}$ 4. $\begin{array}{r}\$1.08 \\ 7\overline{)\$7.56}\end{array}$ 5. $\begin{array}{r}\$2.80 \\ 3\overline{)\$8.40}\end{array}$

6. $\begin{array}{r}\$1.05 \\ 9\overline{)\$9.45}\end{array}$ 7. $\begin{array}{r}\$2.10 \\ 4\overline{)\$8.40}\end{array}$ 8. $\begin{array}{r}\$3.67 \\ 2\overline{)\$7.34}\end{array}$ 9. $\begin{array}{r}\$0.50 \\ 8\overline{)\$4.00}\end{array}$ 10. $\begin{array}{r}\$0.69 \\ 7\overline{)\$4.83}\end{array}$

11. $\begin{array}{r}\$2.80 \\ 6\overline{)\$16.80}\end{array}$ 12. $\begin{array}{r}\$13.29 \\ 4\overline{)\$53.16}\end{array}$ 13. $\begin{array}{r}\$12.06 \\ 5\overline{)\$60.30}\end{array}$ 14. $\begin{array}{r}\$4.01 \\ 8\overline{)\$32.08}\end{array}$ 15. $\begin{array}{r}\$13.20 \\ 7\overline{)\$92.40}\end{array}$

Mixed Applications

16. Clara, Nora, and Sandy earned $22.50 raking leaves. They shared the money equally. How much money did each person get?

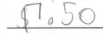
$7.50

17. Jacob bought 4 notebooks. Each one cost the same amount of money. His change from a $10 bill was $0.84. How much did each notebook cost?

$2.29

Meaning of the Remainder

Solve. Tell how you interpret the meaning of the remainder.

1. The 158 fourth graders from the Glenwood School are going on a picnic. If there are 8 hot dogs in a package, how many packages are needed for each student to have 2 hot dogs?

   40 packages

2. Some of the students baked cookies for the picnic. Jeff baked 50 cookies. How many packages of 3 cookies each could he make?

   16 packages

3. The 158 students divide up into teams of 8 for a scavenger hunt. The students who are left over form a smaller team. How many teams are there?

   20 teams

4. Mrs. Jackson bought 7 dozen eggs for an egg-tossing contest. If the 158 students divide into pairs, and each pair of students takes 1 egg, how many eggs are left over?

   5 eggs

Mixed Applications

For Problems 5–7, use the price list.

5. Kito bought 4 pencils, 2 erasers, and a ruler. How much money did he spend?

   _$1.20_

School Store Price List	
Item	Price
Pencil	$0.10
Eraser	$0.15
Ruler	$0.50

6. On Monday, the store sold 20 pencils, 10 erasers, and 3 rulers. On Tuesday, the store sold 15 pencils, 13 erasers, and 3 rulers. On which day did the store take in more money?

   Monday

7. On Friday, the store received a new supply of 72 pencils. Bill arranged the new pencils in groups of 5. How many groups could he make? How many pencils were left over?

   14 groups 2 left over

Problem Solving

Account for All Possibilities

Solve. Account for all the possibilities.

1. There were 86 campers at a summer camp. They divided as evenly as possible into 7 groups for hiking. How many campers were in each group?

   5 groups of 12, 2 groups of 13

2. The camp cook baked 24 dozen cookies. She divided them as equally as possible into 7 boxes. How many cookies did she put into each box?

   6 boxes with 41 cool. 1 box 42 cookies

3. During the evening quiet time at camp, Karen finished a 148-page book in 7 days. If she read about the same number of pages each day, how many pages did she read each day?

   6 days 21 pages and 1 day 22 pages

4. At meal times, the 86 campers and 10 counselors sat at tables that each fit 8 people. What is the fewest number of tables necessary to seat all the campers and counselors?

   12 tables

Mixed Applications

Solve.

CHOOSE A STRATEGY

- Act It Out • Write a Number Sentence • Work Backward • Find a Pattern

5. Dave's *Save the Plains Grass* group collected grass seed in the fall. Each day, they collected twice as many seeds as they collected the day before. The group collected 48 seeds on Friday. How many seeds did they collect on Monday?

   3 seeds

6. Tim has 1 quarter and 4 pennies. Jack has 4 dimes. Barb has 4 nickels and 1 penny. How can they share the coins so that each person has the same amount of money?

   1Q and 1N, 3d, 1d, 3N 5p

Finding the Average

Vocabulary

Complete.

1. An ___Average___ is one way to find a
number that best represents all the numbers in a set.

Find the average of each set of numbers by using unit cubes.

2. 7, 7, 10, 12, 14

   10

3. 3, 5, 6, 9, 12, 13

   8

4. 6, 10, 12, 12

   10

5. 11, 15, 18, 20

   16

6. 7, 11, 14, 14, 14

   12

7. 15, 18, 24

   17

8. Jill bought 5 books at the school book fair. The price of 1 book was $6. The price of 3 books was $3 each. The last book cost $5. What was the average price Jill paid per book?

   $4.00

9. Each morning, Tyler counts the number of cardinals at his bird feeder. Last week he counted 5 cardinals on Monday, 4 on Tuesday, 7 on Wednesday, 2 on Thursday, and 2 on Friday. What was the average number of cardinals Tyler counted each day?

   4 cardinals

Mixed Applications

10. Carrie picked 82 apples. She wants to divide them into 5 bags to share with her friends. How many apples can she put into each bag?

     16 apples in 3 bags
    2 bags 17 apple

11. John is cutting pieces of yarn to make hair for a mask. How many 8-inch pieces of yarn can John cut from a 10-foot long piece of yarn?

    15 pieces

Choosing the Operation

Solve. Name the operation you used.

1. Mr. Murphy owns a bakery. On Saturday, he baked 60 blueberry muffins, 48 corn muffins, and 72 cranberry muffins. How many muffins did he bake in all?

   108 muffins

2. Mr. Murphy sold 498 cookies on Saturday. At the beginning of the day, there were 512 cookies. How many cookies were left at the end of the day?

   IH cookies

3. Susan bought 4 muffins for $0.79 each. How much money did she spend?

   _$3.16_

4. Ryan paid $2.34 for 6 chocolate chip cookies. How much did each cookie cost?

   _39¢_

For Problems 5–7, use the graph.

5. How many bicycles were sold during the week?

   30 bicycles

6. What was the average number of bicycles sold each day?

   5 bicycles

7. How many more bicycles were sold on Saturday than on Monday?

   8 more

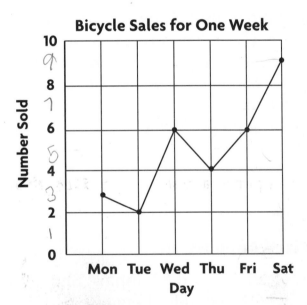

Bicycle Sales for One Week

Number Sold (y-axis: 0 to 10)

Day (x-axis: Mon Tue Wed Thu Fri Sat)

8. Will wants to buy a bicycle that costs $109. He has already saved $45. If Will earns $5 each week, how many weeks will it take him to save enough money to buy the bicycle?

   13 weeks

9. Some days, Mary rides her bicycle to and from school. The distance is about 2 miles each way. In October, Mary rode her bicycle to and from school 14 times. About how many miles did she ride in October?

   56 min.

Fractions: Part of a Whole

Vocabulary

Fill in the blank.

1. A number that names a part of a whole is a __*fractions*__.

_____

Complete the table.

Model	Fraction	Read
	$\frac{2}{5}$	two fifths, two out of five, two divided by five
2.	$\frac{1}{3}$	
3. 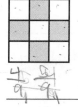	$\frac{1}{2}$	

What fraction is shaded? What fraction is not shaded?

4.

$\frac{2}{5}$ $\frac{3}{5}$

5.

$\frac{3}{4}$ $\frac{1}{4}$

6.

$\frac{4}{5}$ $\frac{1}{5}$

7.

$\frac{4}{9}$ $\frac{5}{9}$

Draw a picture and shade part of it to show the fraction.

8. $\frac{2}{6}$

9. $\frac{7}{8}$

10. $\frac{4}{5}$

$$3.50$$
$$\times \ 12$$
$$17\ 00$$
$$+ 35\ 00$$
$$42.00$$

Mixed Applications

11. Fred ate half the pie. Brian ate
    half of the remaining pie. What
    fraction of the original pie is left?

    $\frac{1}{4}$

12. A magazine costs $3.50 per
    month on the newsstand. A
    12-month subscription costs
    $30.00. How much money is
    saved over a 1-year period if
    you subscribe to the magazine?

    $12.00

Fractions: Part of a Group

What fraction of the parts is shaded? What fraction
is not shaded?

1.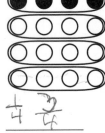

$\frac{1}{4}$ $\frac{3}{4}$

2.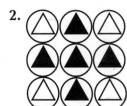

$\frac{5}{9}$ $\frac{4}{9}$

3.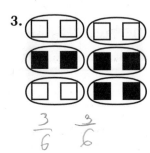

$\frac{3}{6}$ $\frac{3}{6}$

4.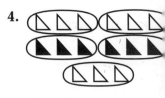

$\frac{2}{5}$ $\frac{3}{5}$

5.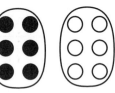

$\frac{1}{2}$ $\frac{1}{2}$

6.

$\frac{7}{8}$ $\frac{1}{8}$

7.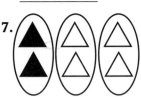

$\frac{1}{3}$ $\frac{2}{3}$

8.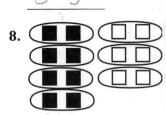

$\frac{4}{7}$ $\frac{3}{7}$

Draw the picture and shade 1 part. Write the fraction for the
shaded area.

9. 12 circles

4 parts $\frac{1}{4}$

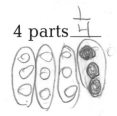

10. 8 triangles

8 parts $\frac{1}{8}$

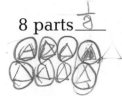

$\frac{1}{5}$

11. 6 stars

2 parts $\frac{1}{2}$

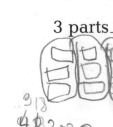

12. 9 squares

3 parts $\frac{1}{3}$

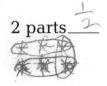

$\begin{array}{r} 9\ 18 \\ 483{,}300{,}000 \\ -\ 93{,}000{,}000 \\ \hline 390{,}300{,}060 \end{array}$

Mixed Applications

13. Mrs. Arturo cut a pizza into
8 equal pieces. Lorenzo ate
5 pieces. What fraction of the
pizza was eaten? What fraction
of the pizza was not eaten?

$\frac{5}{8}$ $\frac{3}{8}$

14. The Earth is approximately
93,000,000 miles from the sun.
Jupiter is about 483,300,000
miles from the sun. What is the
approximate distance in miles
between Earth and Jupiter?

390,300,000 mil.

Equivalent Fractions

Vocabulary

Fill in the blank.

1. Fractions that name the same amount are called
   _____Equivalent_____Fraction_____.

Use fraction bars to model an equivalent fraction for each picture.
Record the fraction.

2.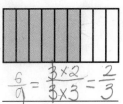

$\frac{6}{9} = \frac{3 \times 2}{3 \times 3} = \frac{2}{3}$

3.

$\frac{4}{8} = \frac{2 \times 2}{4 \times 4 \times 2} = \frac{1}{2}$

4.

$\frac{4}{10} = \frac{2 \times 2}{5 \times 4} = \frac{2}{5}$

Find an equivalent fraction. Use fraction bars.

5. $\frac{1}{4} \cdot \frac{2}{2} = \frac{2}{8}$

6. $\frac{2}{3} = \frac{4}{6}$

7. $\frac{1}{2} = \frac{2}{4}$

8. $\frac{3}{6} = \frac{6}{12}$

9. $\frac{3}{6} = \frac{3}{2 \times 3} = \frac{1}{2}$

10. $\frac{2}{8} = \frac{1}{4}$

11. $\frac{5}{6} = \frac{10}{12}$

12. $\frac{5}{10} = \frac{1}{2}$

13. $\frac{8}{12} = \frac{2 \times 2 \times 2}{2 \times 2 \times 3} = \frac{2}{3}$

14. $\frac{6}{8} = \frac{3}{4}$

15. $\frac{6}{12} = \frac{1}{2}$

16. $\frac{9}{12} = \frac{3}{4}$

17. $\frac{4}{12} = \frac{1}{3}$

18. $\frac{4}{5} = \frac{8}{10}$

19. $\frac{6}{8} = \frac{3}{4}$

20. $\frac{4}{6} = \frac{2}{3}$

Mixed Applications

21. A case of fruit juice contains 4 six-packs. If 3 six-packs were used for a party, what fraction of the fruit juice six-packs remains?

    $\frac{1}{4}$

    _____

22. If a car travels at 55 miles per hour, how many miles will it travel in 6 hours?

    330 miles

    _____

    $\overset{3}{55}$

    $\times \ 6$
    $\overline{330}$

Comparing and Ordering Fractions

Write the fraction for each model. Then compare, using <, >, or =.

1.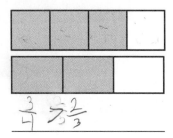

$\frac{3}{4} > \frac{2}{3}$

2.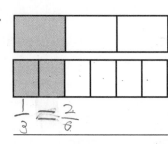

$\frac{1}{3} = \frac{2}{6}$

3.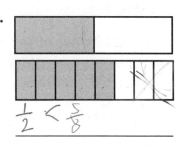

$\frac{1}{2} < \frac{5}{8}$

Compare the fractions. Write <, >, or =. Use fraction bars.

4. $\frac{1}{3}$ ⊘ $\frac{1}{4}$

5. $\frac{5}{6}$ ⊘ $\frac{4}{6}$

6. $\frac{1}{2}$ ⊘ $\frac{6}{12}$

7. $\frac{3}{4}$ ⊘ $\frac{3}{5}$

8. $\frac{2}{5}$ $<$ $\frac{3}{5}$

9. $\frac{1}{8}$ $<$ $\frac{1}{7}$

10. $\frac{2}{4}$ ⊘ $\frac{1}{2}$

11. $\frac{4}{8}$ ⊘ $\frac{4}{10}$

Use fraction bars to order each set of fractions from greatest to least.

12. $\frac{2}{5}, \frac{1}{5}, \frac{3}{5}$

$\frac{3}{5}, \frac{2}{5}, \frac{1}{5}$

13. $\frac{2}{6}, \frac{1}{4}, \frac{2}{5}$

$\frac{2}{5}, \frac{2}{6}, \frac{1}{4}$

14. $\frac{1}{6}, \frac{1}{3}, \frac{1}{2}$

$\frac{1}{2}, \frac{1}{3}, \frac{1}{6}$

15. $\frac{3}{4}, \frac{2}{3}, \frac{5}{8}$

$\frac{3}{4}, \frac{2}{3}, \frac{5}{8}$

Use fraction bars to order each set of fractions from least to greatest.

16. $\frac{3}{12}, \frac{4}{10}, \frac{2}{3}$

$\frac{3}{12}, \frac{4}{10}, \frac{2}{3}$

17. $\frac{5}{8}, \frac{1}{2}, \frac{2}{3}$

$\frac{5}{8}, \frac{1}{2}, \frac{2}{3}$

18. $\frac{1}{4}, \frac{1}{6}, \frac{1}{5}$

$\frac{1}{6}, \frac{1}{5}, \frac{1}{4}$

19. $\frac{4}{6}, \frac{7}{12}, \frac{2}{5}$

$\frac{2}{5}, \frac{4}{6}, \frac{7}{12}$

Mixed Applications

20. Debby used $\frac{1}{2}$ cup of chocolate chips in her cookies. Valerie used $\frac{2}{3}$ cup of chocolate chips in her cookies. Who used the greater amount of chips?

Valerie

21. The total weight of 5 students was 425 pounds. If each student weighed the same amount, how much did each student weigh?

85 lbs.

Problem-Solving Strategy

Make a Model

Make a model to solve.

1. The cafeteria made a punch using $\frac{1}{2}$ gallon of apple juice, $\frac{5}{8}$ gallon of orange juice, and $\frac{2}{3}$ gallon of raspberry juice. List the juices in order from greatest to least.

   _rj, oj, aj,_____

2. A school had 3 music groups, each with 24 students. The choir was made up of $\frac{1}{3}$ boys, the band was $\frac{3}{4}$ boys, and the orchestra was $\frac{5}{8}$ boys. Which music group had the greatest fraction of girls?

   _Choir_____

3. Kyle bought cookies at a bakery. He bought $\frac{1}{2}$ dozen oatmeal cookies, $\frac{2}{3}$ dozen cinnamon cookies, and $\frac{3}{4}$ dozen chocolate cookies. List each part of a dozen cookies in order from greatest to least.

   _Chocolate, Cinnamon, oatmeal_____

4. Katrina made a square design with 25 tiles. She used 9 red tiles for the diagonals, 12 yellow tiles to complete the outside border, and 4 blue tiles to complete the center. Show what Katrina's design looked like.

Mixed Applications

Solve.

CHOOSE A STRATEGY

- Act It Out • Use a Table • Make an Organized List • Guess and Check • Work Backward

5. Karen cuts lawns for $15.00 each. She cut 2 lawns a day for 9 days. Mark baby-sits for $3.25 an hour. He baby-sat five hours a day for 8 days. Who made more money? How much more money?

   _Karen $140 more_____

6. Shari is making a 10-inch by 10-inch checkerboard. She is alternating 1-inch squares of white and purple on the board. How many purple squares will Shari need?

   _50 ps._____

Name _____

Mixed Numbers

Vocabulary

Fill in the blank.

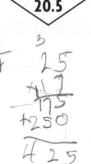

1. A __Mixed Numbers__ is made up of a
   whole number and a fraction.

For Exercises 2–4, use the figures at the right.

2. How many whole figures are shaded?
   Into how many equal parts is each figure divided?

   4, 3

3. How many parts in the fifth figure are shaded?

   2

4. What fraction and mixed number can you write for

   the shaded parts of the figures? __$\frac{14}{3}$) $4\frac{2}{3}$__

Write a mixed number for each picture.

5.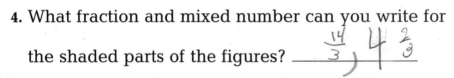

   $2\frac{5}{9}$ $\frac{5}{9}$

6.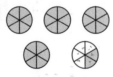

   $4\frac{2}{6}$

7.

   $2\frac{3}{5}$

Rename each fraction as a mixed number. You may wish to draw a picture.

8. $\frac{16}{3}$ $5\frac{+}{3}$ 9. $\frac{9}{2}$ $4\frac{1}{2}$ 10. $\frac{17}{6}$ $2\frac{5}{6}$ 11. $\frac{13}{4}$ $3\frac{1}{4}$

   $6\overline{)17}$

Mixed Applications

12. Mary ate $\frac{1}{4}$ of the pizza, Frank
    ate $\frac{2}{8}$ of the pizza. Did one
    person eat less pizza?

    no!

13. Anne's backyard is 25 feet wide
    and 17 feet long. What is the
    yard's perimeter? its area?

    84 ft. 425 sq. ft.

    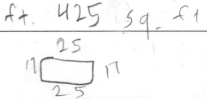

Adding Like Fractions

Use fraction bars to find the sum. Draw the bars.

1. $\frac{3}{6} + \frac{1}{6} =$ $\frac{4}{6}$

2. $\frac{1}{8} + \frac{6}{8} =$ $\frac{7}{8}$

3. $\frac{3}{5} + \frac{4}{5} =$ $\frac{7}{5}$

4. $\frac{5}{12} + \frac{2}{12} =$ $\frac{7}{12}$

5. $\frac{6}{10} + \frac{7}{10} =$ $\frac{13}{10}$

6. $\frac{3}{4} + \frac{2}{4} =$ $\frac{5}{4}$

Write the letter of the number sentence for each model. Find the sum.

7.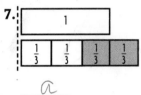

_a_

8.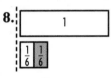

_c_

9.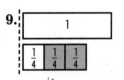

_d_

10.

_b_

a. $\frac{2}{3} + \frac{2}{3} =$ $\frac{4}{3}$

b. $\frac{5}{8} + \frac{1}{8} =$ $\frac{6}{8}$

c. $\frac{1}{6} + \frac{1}{6} =$ $\frac{2}{6}$

d. $\frac{1}{4} + \frac{2}{4} =$ $\frac{3}{4}$

11.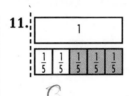

_c_

12.

_b_

13.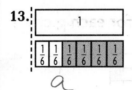

_a_

14.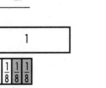

_d_

a. $\frac{2}{6} + \frac{4}{6} =$ $\frac{6}{6}$

b. $\frac{1}{4} + \frac{1}{4} =$ $\frac{2}{4}$

c. $\frac{2}{5} + \frac{3}{5} =$ $\frac{5}{5}$

d. $\frac{3}{8} + \frac{2}{8} =$ $\frac{5}{8}$

Mixed Applications

15. Twenty-four people were asked their favorite type of movie. Ten people liked adventures, five liked romances, and nine liked science fiction. What fraction of the people surveyed liked science fiction? $\frac{9}{24}$

16. You baked a pie and cut it into 8 pieces. After dinner your family ate $\frac{3}{8}$ of the pie. Later, some friends came over and they ate $\frac{4}{8}$ of the pie. How much of the pie was eaten? $\frac{7}{8}$

More About Adding Like Fractions

Write a number sentence for each problem and then find the sum.

1. one fourth plus two fourths

$\frac{1}{4} + \frac{2}{4} = \frac{3}{4}$

2. two fifths plus one fifth

$\frac{2}{5} + \frac{1}{5} = \frac{3}{5}$

3. three sixths plus two sixths

$\frac{3}{6} + \frac{2}{6} = \frac{5}{6}$

4. five eighths plus four eighths

$\frac{5}{8} + \frac{4}{8} = \frac{9}{8}$

5. three fourths plus three fourths

$\frac{3}{4} + \frac{3}{4} = \frac{6}{4}$

6. five ninths plus six ninths

$\frac{5}{9} + \frac{6}{9} = \frac{11}{9}$

7. two eighths plus three eighths

$\frac{2}{8} + \frac{3}{8} = \frac{5}{8}$

8. one half plus one half

$\frac{1}{2} + \frac{1}{2} = \frac{2}{2}$

Find the sum.

9. $\frac{1}{6} + \frac{2}{6} = \frac{3}{6}$

10. $\frac{3}{12} + \frac{5}{12} = \frac{8}{12}$

11. $\frac{5}{8} + \frac{2}{8} = \frac{7}{8}$

12. $\frac{1}{3} + \frac{2}{3} = \frac{3}{3}$

13. $\frac{4}{10} + \frac{5}{10} = \frac{9}{10}$

14. $\frac{3}{7} + \frac{1}{7} = \frac{4}{7}$

15. $\frac{1}{5} + \frac{4}{5} = \frac{5}{5}$

16. $\frac{1}{12} + \frac{9}{12} = \frac{10}{12}$

17. $\frac{6}{9} + \frac{2}{9} = \frac{8}{9}$

Mixed Applications

18. At the start of recess, $\frac{3}{8}$ of the class played on the swings. They were joined by $\frac{2}{8}$ of the class. What fraction of the class played on the swings?

$\frac{5}{8}$

19. Alexander jogs every day after school. On Monday he jogged $\frac{2}{8}$ of a mile. On Tuesday he jogged $\frac{5}{8}$ of a mile. How much has he jogged so far this week?

$\frac{7}{8}$ miles

20. Morgan wants to save cans. She saved 24 cans the first week. She saved 18 cans the second week. The third week she saved 38 cans. How many cans has Morgan saved?

$\begin{array}{r} 18 \\ 24 \\ + 38 \\ \hline 80 \end{array}$

80 cans

21. In the classroom there are 7 rows of chairs. Each row has 6 chairs. How many students can sit in the chairs?

43 students

Subtracting Like Fractions

Use fraction bars or paper folding to find the difference.
Draw a picture and write the difference.

1. $\dfrac{3}{4} - \dfrac{2}{4} =$ $\dfrac{1}{4}$

2. $\dfrac{4}{6} - \dfrac{3}{6} =$ $\dfrac{1}{6}$

3. $\dfrac{7}{8} - \dfrac{3}{8} =$ $\dfrac{4}{8}$

4. $\dfrac{5}{10} - \dfrac{3}{10} =$ $\dfrac{2}{10}$

5. $\dfrac{3}{5} - \dfrac{1}{5} =$ $\dfrac{2}{5}$

6. $\dfrac{6}{8} - \dfrac{2}{8} =$ $\dfrac{4}{8}$

7. $\dfrac{10}{12} - \dfrac{5}{12} =$ $\dfrac{5}{12}$

8. $\dfrac{7}{10} - \dfrac{3}{10} =$ $\dfrac{4}{10}$

9. $\dfrac{5}{6} - \dfrac{1}{6} =$ $\dfrac{4}{6}$

Write the letter of the number sentence for each model.
Find the difference.

10.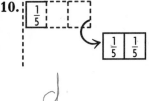

_d_

11.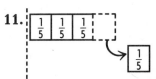

_c_

12.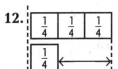

_a_

13.

_b_

$\begin{array}{r} 12 \\ 11 \\ + 8 \\ \hline 31 \end{array}$

a. $\dfrac{3}{4} - \dfrac{1}{4} =$ $\dfrac{2}{4}$

b. $\dfrac{2}{4} - \dfrac{1}{4} =$ $\dfrac{1}{4}$

c. $\dfrac{4}{5} - \dfrac{1}{5} =$ $\dfrac{3}{5}$

d. $\dfrac{3}{5} - \dfrac{2}{5} =$ $\dfrac{1}{5}$

Mixed Applications

14. Rudy brought $\dfrac{7}{8}$ of a pie to share with his friends. His friends ate $\dfrac{5}{8}$ of the pie. How much of the pie did he have left?

$\dfrac{2}{8}$

$\dfrac{7}{8} - \dfrac{5}{8} = \dfrac{2}{8}$

15. On a recent shopping trip, John bought gifts for his family. He spent $8 on his father. His mother's present cost $11. He spent $3 on each of his 4 brothers. How much money did he spend?

$31.00

Problem-Solving Strategy

Make a Model

Make a model to solve.

1. Henry and Sue each ate $\frac{1}{3}$ of a small cake. What fraction of the cake was left?

    $\frac{1}{3}$

2. Linda baked a huge cookie for her friends. Sue and Mary each ate $\frac{1}{4}$ of the cookie. How much was left for Linda?

    $\frac{2}{4}$

3. Phillip likes to ride his bike, skateboard and read in his spare time. He spends $\frac{2}{8}$ of his time riding his bike and $\frac{5}{8}$ of his time skateboarding. How much of his spare time does he have left to spend reading?

    $\frac{1}{8}$

4. Mr. Jones baked 12 cupcakes for the class party. Before lunch $\frac{3}{12}$ of the cupcakes were eaten. After lunch $\frac{5}{12}$ of the cupcakes were eaten. What fraction of the cupcakes were left for a snack after school?

    $\frac{4}{12}$

Mixed Applications

Solve.

CHOOSE A STRATEGY

• **Act It Out** • **Use a Table** • **Make an Organized List** • **Guess and Check**

5. At the end of five days Henry had saved $30. If each day he saved $2 more than the day before, how much money did Henry save each day?

    D1 $2, D2 $4, D3 $6, D4 $8, D5 $10

6. Mrs. Gonzales used $\frac{3}{8}$ of a piece of material to make a mask and $\frac{2}{8}$ for a belt. What fraction of the material is left to make a hat?

    $\frac{3}{8}$

7. In a word game using letter tiles, Lilly chooses two letters from these four remaining letters: P, R, S, and T. List all the possible choices.

    PR, PS, PT, RS, RT, TS

8. A series of numbers starts with $\frac{1}{4}$. Each number in the series is two times greater than the number before it. What is the sixth number in the series?

    8

Adding Mixed Numbers

Find the sum.

1. $1\frac{2}{5}$
$+3\frac{1}{5}$
$4\frac{3}{5}$

2. $3\frac{2}{6}$
$+2\frac{3}{6}$
$5\frac{5}{6}$

3. $2\frac{4}{9}$
$+6\frac{2}{9}$
$8\frac{6}{9}$

4. $5\frac{3}{8}$
$+1\frac{3}{8}$
$6\frac{8}{8}$

5. $3\frac{4}{10}$
$+5\frac{1}{10}$
$8\frac{5}{10}$

6. $7\frac{1}{4}$
$+4\frac{2}{4}$
$11\frac{3}{4}$

7. $5\frac{1}{3}$
$+2\frac{1}{3}$
$7\frac{2}{3}$

8. $8\frac{5}{12}$
$+1\frac{4}{12}$
$9\frac{9}{12}$

9. $7\frac{2}{6}$
$+6\frac{4}{6}$
$13\frac{6}{6}$

10. $9\frac{5}{8}$
$+5\frac{4}{8}$
$15\frac{1}{8}$

11. $5\frac{3}{4}$
$+2\frac{3}{4}$
$8\frac{2}{4}$

12. $3\frac{4}{5}$
$+6\frac{2}{5}$
$10\frac{1}{5}$

13. $3\frac{2}{5} + 4\frac{1}{5} =$ $7\frac{3}{5}$

14. $4\frac{2}{6} + 3\frac{1}{6} =$ $7\frac{3}{6}$

15. $8\frac{3}{10} + 4\frac{5}{10} =$ $12\frac{8}{10}$

16. $9\frac{4}{8} + 6\frac{2}{8} =$ $15\frac{6}{8}$

17. $8\frac{2}{3} + 4\frac{1}{3} =$ $12\frac{3}{3}$

18. $4\frac{7}{9} + 2\frac{5}{9} =$ $7\frac{3}{9}$

Mixed Applications

19. Two friends are making a large sign. They each have a strip of paper $3\frac{2}{8}$ feet long. If they put their paper together with no overlap, how long will the sign be?

$6\frac{4}{8}$

20. To get ready for her math test, Celeste decided to study for two days. On Thursday she studied for 1 hour and 35 minutes and on Friday for 1 hour and 25 minutes. How much time did she spend studying?

3 hours

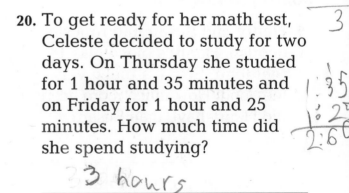

21. A recipe for punch calls for adding $2\frac{3}{4}$ quarts of water to $1\frac{1}{4}$ quarts of fruit juice. How many quarts of punch will you have when you mix the two?

$3\frac{4}{4}$

Subtracting Mixed Numbers

Find the difference.

(handwritten in top margin)
$15 \times 4 = 60$

1. $5\frac{7}{8}$
$-2\frac{3}{8}$
_____
$3\frac{4}{8}$

2. $6\frac{4}{10}$
$-4\frac{3}{10}$
_____
$2\frac{1}{10}$

3. $9\frac{3}{4}$
$-2\frac{2}{4}$
_____
$7\frac{1}{4}$

4. $3\frac{2}{3}$
$-2\frac{1}{3}$
_____
$1\frac{1}{3}$

5. $5\frac{4}{5}$
$-1\frac{2}{5}$
_____
$4\frac{2}{5}$

6. $8\frac{6}{8}$
$-3\frac{2}{8}$
_____
$5\frac{4}{8}$

7. $9\frac{8}{12}$
$-6\frac{4}{12}$
_____
$3\frac{4}{12}$

8. $4\frac{5}{6}$
$-3\frac{3}{6}$
_____
$1\frac{2}{6}$

9. $7\frac{8}{9}$
$-6\frac{1}{9}$
_____
$1\frac{7}{9}$

10. $9\frac{9}{10}$
$-5\frac{2}{10}$
_____
$4\frac{7}{10}$

11. $8\frac{2}{4}$
$-6\frac{1}{4}$
_____
$2\frac{1}{4}$

12. $3\frac{10}{12}$
$-1\frac{7}{12}$
_____
$2\frac{3}{12}$

13. $7\frac{4}{5} - 1\frac{3}{5} = 6\frac{1}{5}$

14. $9\frac{5}{8} - 4\frac{4}{8} = 5\frac{1}{8}$

15. $4\frac{6}{9} - 2\frac{2}{9} = 2\frac{4}{9}$

16. $5\frac{9}{12} - 2\frac{3}{12} = 2\frac{6}{12}$

17. $9\frac{2}{5} - 3\frac{1}{5} = 6\frac{1}{5}$

18. $6\frac{7}{10} - 2\frac{5}{10} = 4\frac{2}{10}$

Mixed Applications

19. Henry and Susan had ropes of licorice. Henry's piece was $1\frac{3}{4}$ feet long. Susan's piece was $1\frac{1}{4}$ feet long. How much more licorice did Henry have than Susan?

$\frac{2}{4}$

_____

20. The school trip is being planned. There are 15 students going from 4 different classrooms. How many students are planning on going?

60 students

_____

21. The jumping contest allowed everyone to make two standing broad jumps and then enter the total distance of the two jumps. Cindy made a jump of $3\frac{3}{8}$ feet and one of $2\frac{6}{8}$ feet. What was the total of her two jumps?

$6\frac{1}{8}$

_____

22. Rico wanted to time himself walking to his new school. He left his house at 8:35 A.M. He arrived at the school at 9:20 A.M. How long did it take him to walk to school?

55 min.

_____

(handwritten at left margin)
1. $3\frac{3}{8}$
2. $2\frac{6}{8}$
___
$\frac{1}{8}$

Name _____

Relating Fractions and Decimals

Vocabulary

Complete.

1. A ___Decimal___ is a number that uses place value and a decimal point to show a value less than one, such as tenths and hundredths.

Write the decimal for the part that is shaded.

2.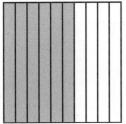

___0.6___

3.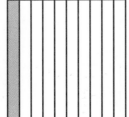

___0.1___

4.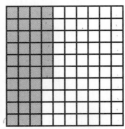

___0.36___

5.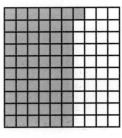

___0.61___

Write each fraction as a decimal.

6. $\frac{6}{10}$ _0.6_

7. $\frac{8}{10}$ _0.8_

8. $\frac{39}{100}$ _0.39_

9. $\frac{64}{100}$ _0.64_

Write each decimal as a fraction.

10. 0.2 _$\frac{2}{10}$_

11. 0.4 _$\frac{4}{10}$_

12. 0.12 _$\frac{12}{100}$_

13. 0.66 _$\frac{66}{100}$_

Mixed Applications

14. Jane answered 8 out of 10 problems correctly on her math test. Write a fraction and a decimal to show how many problems Jane got right.

___0.8, $\frac{8}{10}$___

15. Derek gave $\frac{1}{2}$ of his energy bar to Sam and $\frac{1}{4}$ to Sandy. How much of his energy bar does Derek have left?

___$\frac{1}{4}$___

16. During his vacation, Brian used 7 rolls of 24-photo film. How many photos did Brian take?

___168 photos___

17. If 8 students can sit at one table, how many tables are needed to seat 134 students?

___17 tables___

Tenths and Hundredths

Write the amount as a fraction of a dollar, a decimal, and a money amount.

1. 17 pennies
$\frac{17}{100}$

0.17

$0.17

2. 38 pennies
$\frac{38}{100}$

0.38

$0.38

3. 5 dimes
$\frac{50}{100}$

0.50

$0.50

4. 9 dimes
$\frac{90}{100}$

0.90

$0.90

Write the decimal and the decimal name for the shaded part of each model.

5.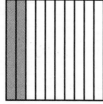

0.2

two tenths

6.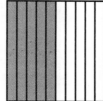

0.5

five tenths

7.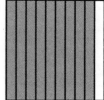

0.9

nine tenths

8.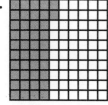

0.42

forty two hundredths

9.

0.35

thirty-five hundredths

10.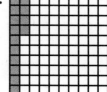

0.14

fourteen hundredths

Mixed Applications

11. Jessica bought a popsicle for $0.45. What fraction of a dollar is Jessica's change from a $1 bill?

$\frac{55}{100}$

12. Nancy has a collection of 10 beads. Two-tenths of the beads are red and the rest are white. Write the number of white beads as a fraction and as a decimal.

$\frac{8}{10}$ 0.8

Equivalent Decimals

Vocabulary

Complete.

1. _Equivalent decimals_ are different names for the
same amount.

Write an equivalent decimal for each. You may wish to use
decimal models.

2. 0.7   3. 0.1   4. 0.60   5. 0.4   6. 0.20

   0.70   0.10   0.6   0.40   0.2

7. 0.8   8. 0.30   9. 0.5   10. 0.90   11. 0.3

   0.80   0.30   0.50   0.9   0.30

Are the two decimals equivalent? Write *yes* or *no*.

12. 0.4 and 0.40 __yes__   13. 0.1 and 0.01 __no__

14. 0.50 and 0.5 __yes__   15. 0.20 and 0.02 __no__

16. 0.3 and 0.30 __yes__   17. 0.80 and 0.8 __yes__

18. 0.9 and 0.90 __yes__   19. 0.18 and 0.81 __no__

Mixed Applications

20. Peter has 4 tenths of a dollar,
Tamara has 30 hundredths of a
dollar, and Jon has $0.50.

   a. Who has the most money?

   Jon

   b. Who has the least money?

   Tamara

21. Clay's walk to school is 0.4 mile.

   a. Write this decimal as a fraction.

   $\frac{4}{10}$

   b. Is Clay's walk greater than or
   less than half a mile?

   less than

Comparing and Ordering

Tell which number is greater.

1.	0.45	2.	0.4	3.	0.90	4.	0.60	5.	0.06
	0.35		0.6		0.91		0.64		0.60

1. <u>0.45</u> 2. <u>0.6</u> 3. <u>0.91</u> 4. <u>0.64</u> 5. <u>0.60</u>

6.	0.50	7.	0.7	8.	0.02	9.	0.49	10.	0.80
	0.55		0.17		0.22		0.4		0.79

6. <u>0.55</u> 7. <u>0.7</u> 8. <u>0.22</u> 9. <u>0.49</u> 10. <u>0.80</u>

11.	0.32	12.	0.46	13.	0.25	14.	0.02	15.	0.29
	0.23		0.47		0.2		0.22		0.30

11. <u>0.32</u> 12. <u>0.47</u> 13. <u>0.25</u> 14. <u>0.22</u> 15. <u>(0.30)</u>

Use the number line to order the decimals from greatest to least.

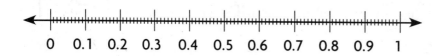

16. 0.45, 0.54, 0.40, 0.04

<u>0.54, 0.45, 0.40, 0.04</u>

17. 0.4, 0.5, 0.04, 0.05, 0.45

<u>0.50, 0.45, 0.4, 0.05, 0.0</u>

18. 0.13, 0.31, 0.3, 0.01, 0.03

<u>0.31, 0.3, 0.13, 0.03, 0.01</u>

19. 0.67, 0.7, 0.76, 0.07, 0.60

<u>0.76, 0.7, 0.67, 0.6, 0.07</u>

20. 0.14, 0.24, 0.20, 0.21, 0.04

<u>0.24, 0.21, 0.20, 0.14, 0.04</u>

21. 0.19, 0.20, 0.1, 0.09, 0.29

<u>0.29, 0.20, 0.19, 0.1, 0.0</u>

Mixed Applications

22. The gift shop sold 5 different kinds of pencils that cost $0.50, $0.35, $0.10, $0.25, and $0.75. Write the amounts in order from the least to the greatest.

<u>$0.10, $0.25, $0.35,</u>
<u>$0.50, $0.75</u>

23. John paid $0.75 each for 2 pens. What is the amount of change he received from $5.00?

1.50 $3.50

Name _____

Mixed Decimals

5.4

Vocabulary

1. Write the letter of the example that is a mixed decimal. ___d___

   a. $\frac{2}{10}$ and $\frac{20}{100}$ b. $2\frac{2}{3}$ c. 0.20 and 0.2   d. 3.45

Write a mixed decimal for each model.

2.

   _1.3_

3.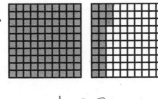

   _1.23_

4.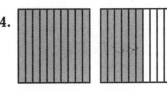

   _1.6_

Write two equivalent mixed decimals for each model.

5.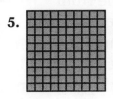

   _2.40, 2.4_

6.

   _2.90, 2.9_

Write each mixed number as a mixed decimal.

7. $4\frac{3}{10}$ _4.3_   8. $6\frac{1}{10}$ _6.1_   9. $2\frac{3}{100}$ _2.033_   10. $4\frac{56}{100}$ _4.56_

Write each mixed decimal as a mixed number.

11. 2.46 _$2\frac{46}{100}$_   12. 1.5 _$1\frac{5}{10}$_   13. 7.99 _$7\frac{99}{100}$_   14. 3.4 _$3\frac{4}{10}$_

Write an equivalent mixed decimal for each.

15. 3.2 _3.20_   16. 6.90 _6.9_   17. 2.20 _2.2_   18. 8.7 _8.70_

Mixed Applications

19. John hiked 2.3 miles on Monday and $2\frac{1}{2}$ miles on Tuesday. On which day did he hike farther?

   Tuesday

20. Tony has read 45 out of the 100 pages in his book. Write a fraction and a decimal to show how much of the book Tony has read.

   $\frac{45}{100}$ 0.45

Name _Kenney_

Problem-Solving Strategy

Make a Table

Make a table to solve.

1. The number of inches of rainfall for Washington, D.C. was 3.10 inches in April, 4.0 inches in May, 3.9 inches in June, and 3.5 inches in July. During which month did it rain the most? the least?

May, April

2. The three runners with the fastest times in the 200-meter run advanced to the finals. Which of the following runners advanced to the finals? Walter finished the race in 22.2 sec; Robert, 24.3 sec; Henry, 23.9 sec; Joe, 25.0 sec; Tommie, 22.1 sec; and Donald, 25.1 sec.

Tommie, Walter, Henry

3. Paula, Ingrid, and Kim went shopping for school supplies. Paula bought three small notebooks for $0.89 each. Kim bought a large notebook for $2.25. Ingrid bought an assignment pad for $0.79 and a set of pens for $1.59. Who spent the most money?

paula

4. Sam had to stay home from school because he had a fever. On Tuesday, his temperature was 99.9 degrees; Wednesday, 101.3; Thursday, 100.5; Friday, 99.0; and Saturday, 98.6. On what day was his temperature the highest?

wednesday

Mixed Applications

Solve.

┌─────── CHOOSE A STRATEGY ───────┐

• **Make a Table**   • **Find a Pattern**   • **Make a Model**   • **Work Backward**

5. In a diving competition, Dorothy got 33.93 points; Pat, 32.67; Elizabeth, 35.45; Greta, 39.90; and Ming, 34.08. Who came in third in the competition?

ming

6. The perimeter of a rectangle is 20 inches, and the width is 2 inches. What is the area of the rectangle?

16 sq inches

Modeling Addition and Subtraction

Use decimal squares to find the sum or difference.

1. $0.2 + 0.4 = n$
0.6

2. $0.5 - 0.1 = n$
0.4

3. $0.87 - 0.42 = n$
0.45

4. $0.46 + 0.32 = n$
0.78

5. $0.7 + 0.2 = n$
0.9

6. $0.8 - 0.6 = n$
0.2

7. $0.59 - 0.16 = n$
0.43

8. $0.62 + 0.28 = n$
0-90

9. $0.3 + 0.5 = n$
0.8

10. $0.3 - 0.2 = n$
0-1

11. $0.34 - 0.14 = n$
0.2

12. $0.15 + 0.56 = n$
0.71

13. $0.1 + 0.6 = n$
0-7

14. $0.9 - 0.3 = n$
0-6

15. $0.95 - 0.45 = n$
0.5

16. $0.38 + 0.50 = n$
0-88

17. $0.5 + 0.2 = n$
0.7

18. $0.4 - 0.2 = n$
0.2

19. $0.62 - 0.21 = n$
0.41

20. $0.64 + 0.11 = n$
0.75

21. $0.2 + 0.1 = n$
0-3

22. $0.7 - 0.1 = n$
0.6

23. $0.77 - 0.54 = n$
0.23

24. $0.24 + 0.39 = n$
0.63

Mixed Applications

25. Peter and Rhonda both started with the same amount of water. At the end of the day, Peter had 0.3 liters of water and Rhonda had 0.6 liters. Who had more water at the end of the day? How much more?

Rhonda, 3o morz

26. Cindy made a stack of oranges. It was 3 layers tall. On the bottom layer there were 20 oranges. On the next layer there were 15 oranges. On the top layer there were 10 oranges. How many oranges were in the stack?

45 oranges

27. Tom can hop on one leg for 0.65 km. Jerry can hop on one leg for 0.85 km. If Tom starts hopping at the place where Jerry finishes, how far do they both hop?

1. 5 Km

28. Alice works for her parents around the house. She gets paid $2 a week as an allowance. There are 52 weeks in a year. How much money does Alice make in a year?

$104

Name _____

Adding Decimals

Write the letter of the model that matches each problem. Solve.

A. 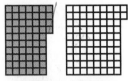 B. 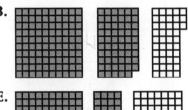 C.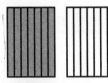

D. 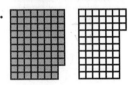 E. 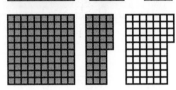 F.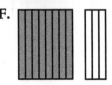

1. $1.35 + 0.64 = n$

_____E_____

2. $0.7 + 0.6 = n$

_____C_____

3. $0.64 + 0.82 = n$

_____a_____

4. $1.59 + 0.43 = n$

_____B_____

5. $0.8 + 0.3 = n$

_____E_____

6. $0.78 + 0.63 = n$

_____D_____

Find the sum.

7. $\begin{array}{r} 0.6 \\ +0.8 \\ \hline 1.4 \end{array}$

8. $\begin{array}{r} 0.52 \\ +0.39 \\ \hline 0.91 \end{array}$

9. $\begin{array}{r} 0.24 \\ +0.36 \\ \hline 0.60 \end{array}$

10. $\begin{array}{r} 0.59 \\ +0.79 \\ \hline 1.38 \end{array}$

11. $\begin{array}{r} 0.72 \\ +0.88 \\ \hline 1.60 \end{array}$

12. $\begin{array}{r} 0.9 \\ +0.9 \\ \hline 1.8 \end{array}$

13. $\begin{array}{r} 0.91 \\ +0.57 \\ \hline 1.48 \end{array}$

14. $\begin{array}{r} 0.88 \\ +0.43 \\ \hline 1.31 \end{array}$

15. $\begin{array}{r} 1.51 \\ +1.80 \\ \hline 3.31 \end{array}$

16. $\begin{array}{r} 1.94 \\ +0.28 \\ \hline 2.22 \end{array}$

Mixed Applications

17. Sally bought two packages of hamburger. One package was 2.45 pounds and the other was 3.16 pounds. How many pounds of hamburger did she buy?

_____5.61_____

18. Carrie started mowing the lawn at 3:45 P.M. and finished at 6:45 P.M. She was paid $12. How much money per hour did she make?

_____$4._____

19. Henry wanted to buy his friends a treat. He had $3.87. If the treat cost $2.65, how much money did he have left?

_____$1.22_____

20. Henry was born on January 15th, 1990, and his friend was born on January 28th, 1990. Who is older? How much older?

_____Henry   13 days old_____

Subtracting Decimals

Write the letter of the model that matches each problem. Solve.

A. 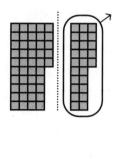 **B.** 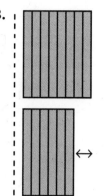 **C.** 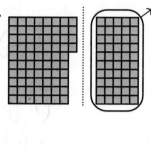 **D.**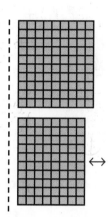

1. $0.8 - 0.6 = n$

_B_ 0.2

2. $0.90 - 0.80 = n$

_D_ 0.10

3. $0.45 - 0.25 = n$

_a_ 0.20

4. $0.74 - 0.50 = n$

_C_ 0.24

Find the difference.

5. 0.9
    -0.2
    $\overline{0.7}$

6. 0.64
    -0.34
    $\overline{0.3}$

7. 1.8
    -0.3
    $\overline{0.5}$

8. 1.36
    -0.76
    $\overline{0.6}$

9. 1.25
    -0.76
    $\overline{0.49}$

10. 1.00
     -0.56
     $\overline{0.44}$

11. 1.62
     -0.73
     $\overline{0.89}$

12. 1.37
     -0.94
     $\overline{0.43}$

13. 1.21
     -0.47
     $\overline{0.74}$

14. 1.16
     -0.64
     $\overline{0.52}$

Mixed Applications

15. The customer wanted to buy 1.50 pounds of Kashi salad. The deli clerk weighed out 1.67 pounds. Was this too much or not enough? Explain.

too much

16. In a bag are 5 peanut bars and 3 bags of chewy bears. What is the probability of reaching into the bag and getting a peanut bar?

$\frac{5}{8}$

17. The school just bought 90 balls for recess. The balls must be shared equally among the 6 classes. How many balls does each class get at recess?

15 Balls

18. Joan's older sister is 1.65 meters tall. Joan is 1.26 meters tall. How much taller is her sister?

0.39

Name _____

Using Decimals

Find the sum.

1.   0.1
  +0.3
   0.4

2.   0.61
  +0.27
   0.88

3.   0.84
  +0.66
   1.50

4.   1.27
  +0.46
   1.73

5.   1.82
  +0.50
   2.32

6.   0.6
  +0.6
   1.2

7.   1.68
  +0.32
   2.00

8.   2.61
  +1.75
   4.36

9.   5.42
  +1.73
   7.15

10.   7.18
  +2.49

Find the difference.

11.   0.5
  −0.2
   0.3

12.   0.6
  −0.3
   0.3

13.   0.37
  −0.15
   0.22

14.   0.54
  −0.36
   0.18

15.   1.60
  −0.06
   1.54

16.   1.31
  −0.27
   0.04

17.   1.15
  −0.31
   0.84

18.   2.47
  −1.26
   1.21

19.   4.82
  −2.76
   2.06

20.   7.19
  −3.44
   3.85

Mixed Applications

21. David entered a 2.4-km walk to raise money for charity. He has already walked 1.7 km. How much farther does he have to walk?

0.7 km

22. Sylvia ran 50 meters in 9.62 seconds. Linda finished 0.35 seconds later. What was Linda's time?

9.97 seconds

23. Sue and Bill collected caterpillars. Sue found one that was 4.7 cm long. Bill found one that was 3.8 cm long. Who found the longer caterpillar? How much longer was it?

Sue 0.9 cm longer

24. Henry bought radish, tomato, and pumpkin seed packages. The radish and tomato seed packages were $0.89 each. The pumpkin seed packages were $1.25 each. How many of each package of seeds did he buy if he spent $4.28 in all?

_____

_____

Problem-Solving Strategy

Write a Number Sentence

Write a number sentence to solve.

1. Morgan batted in runners all 5 times at bat. The first 2 times at bat she batted in 2 runners each time. The last 3 times at bat she batted in 1 runner each time. How many runners did she bat in?

   _____

2. Phillip, George, and Michael were in a relay race. Phillip ran his part in 13.76 seconds, George in 11.32 seconds, and Michael in 9.78 seconds. What was their total time?

   _____

3. Susan practiced shooting free throws for 3 hours. If she shot 50 free throws each hour, how many did she shoot during the entire practice?

   _____

4. The bicyclist weighed each item he had. His helmet weighed 1.1 kilograms. His jacket weighed 0.8 kilogram and his water bottle weighed 2.3 kilograms. What was the total weight of these items?

   _____

Mixed Applications

Solve.

CHOOSE A STRATEGY

- Write a Number Sentence   • Guess and Check   • Make a Table   • Make a Model

5. There are 9 coins equaling $1.40 in a jar. The coins are quarters, dimes, and nickels. How many of each coin are there?

   _____

6. By how much would Funny-Bones have to increase sales to match Silly-Parts sales in February?

   _____

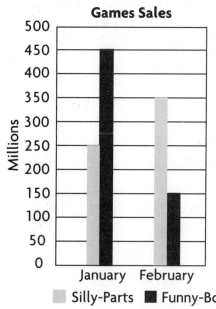

Games Sales

Estimating Sums and Differences by Rounding

Estimate the sum or difference by rounding to the nearest whole number.

1.	1.5 +1.2	2.	1.8 −0.6	3.	2.3 −0.7	4.	2.9 −1.1	5.	3.4 +2.7

6.	4.2 −0.8	7.	6.4 −2.6	8.	2.4 1.9 +2.1	9.	1.7 4.8 +0.4	10.	5.2 1.3 +3.7

Estimate the sum or difference by rounding to the nearest tenth.

11.	1.62 −1.34	12.	3.72 −1.65	13.	2.36 −1.74	14.	3.92 −1.69	15.	3.45 +2.07

16.	3.41 −1.20	17.	2.53 +1.56	18.	3.04 −1.26	19.	2.82 +2.35	20.	4.26 −2.39

Mixed Applications

For Problems 21–23, use the table.

21. Charley practiced punting the football. Each day he punted the ball, his friend Sarah would record his longest punt in air time. On which day did he have the longest time? the shortest time?

Punt Time in Air	
Monday	3.4 seconds
Tuesday	2.5 seconds
Wednesday	1.7 seconds
Thursday	2.8 seconds
Friday	4.2 seconds

_____

22. If you rounded all of the punt air times to the nearest second, what would be the time that occurred most often?

_____

23. Estimate the difference between Charley's longest time and his shortest time.

_____

Linear Measures

Vocabulary

Complete.

1. Measuring length, width, height, and distance are all

   forms of _____ measurement.

2. A(n) _____ is about the length of a baseball bat.

3. A(n) _____ is about the distance you can walk in 20 minutes.

4. A(n) _____ is about the height of a cat.

5. A(n) _____ is about the length of your thumb
   from the first knuckle to the tip.

Choose the reasonable unit of measure. Write *in.*, *ft*, *yd*, or *mi*.

6. The length of a calculator is about 4 _____.

7. The height of a flagpole is about 25 _____.

8. The height of a refrigerator is about 2 _____.

9. The distance along the walkathon is 12 _____.

Name the longer measurement.

10. 50 ft or 50 yd   11. 17 mi or 17 yd   12. 24 in. or 24 yd

_____   _____   _____

Mixed Applications

13. Leon wants to measure the
    length of his bookshelf. Which
    linear units of measure would be
    reasonable to record the length?

14. Write a problem about some-
    thing in your house that can be
    measured. Ask what linear
    measure should be used.

Changing Units

Choose a word from the box that makes each statement true.

1. When you change inches to feet, you _____.

2. When you change inches to miles, you _____.

3. When you change yards to feet, you _____.

4. There are 12 _____ in 1 foot.

5. There are 27 _____ in 9 yards.

6. There are 1,760 _____ in 1 mile.

| inches |
| multiply |
| miles |
| feet |
| divide |
| yards |

Change the unit. You may use a calculator.

7. 48 in. = _____ ft   8. 36 ft = _____ yd   9. 4 yd = _____ in.

10. 3 mi = _____ ft   11. 3,520 yd = _____ mi   12. 5 mi = _____ ft

13. 7 ft = _____ in.   14. 300 ft = _____ yd   15. 432 in. = _____ yd

Mixed Applications

16. To make a bench for their play-house, the children need a board 75 inches long. They have a board that is 6 feet long. Is the board long enough? Explain.

_____

_____

17. To improve his fitness, John decided to walk a mile a week. If he walks five days a week, how many yards does he need to walk each day?

_____

_____

18. Taran's garden is 12 ft long by 6 ft wide. What is the perimeter of the garden in feet? yards? inches?

_____

19. If fencing is $2 a foot, how much would it cost to fence Taran's garden?

_____

Problem-Solving Strategy

Draw a Diagram

Draw a diagram to solve.

1. Sid wants to put plants around his gazebo. It sits on a square shaped piece of concrete. It is 7 feet long on each side. If he puts a plant every foot and one on each of the four corners, how many plants does he need?

2. Ted is putting in a 5-foot-long fence. The colored fence pieces are each 3 inches wide and are set side by side. Ted puts the fence pieces in a red, white, and blue pattern. What color will the final fence piece be?

_____

3. The front of Larry's new coat has buttons every 4 inches. The first button is 2 inches from the top. If the front of the coat is 3 feet long, how many buttons are there?

4. How many cuts do you make when you cut an 8-foot-long board into 1-foot-long pieces?

_____

Mixed Applications

Solve.

CHOOSE A STRATEGY

- **Use a Table**
- **Act It Out**
- **Make an Organized List**
- **Work Backward**

5. In 1936 Jesse Owens ran the 100-meter race in 10.3 seconds. In 1896 Thomas Burke ran the 100-meter race in 12 seconds. How much faster did Jesse Owens run the race?

6. Henry collected 10 cans in the first hour, 15 cans the second hour, and 20 cans the third hour. If this pattern continues, how many cans will he collect in all in six hours?

_____

7. Describe the geometric figure that would come next in this pattern.

8. Along the 30-foot wall, there is a plant every 6 feet. The plants start at one end of the wall. How many plants are there?

_____

Fractions in Measurements

Measure the length of each item to the nearest $\frac{1}{4}$ in.

1.

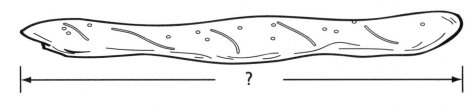

?

_____

2.

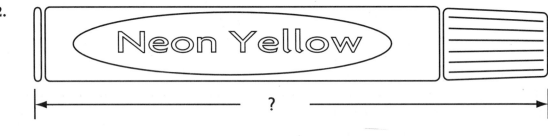

Neon Yellow

?

_____

3.

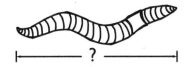

?

_____

Mixed Applications

For Problems 4–5, use the tree chart.

4. To the nearest foot, how tall was the tree in the first year? second year? third year? fourth year?

_____

5. Between which two years did the tree grow the most?

_____

_____

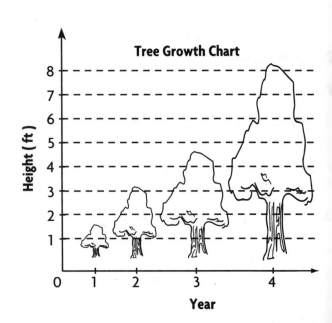

Tree Growth Chart

Name _____

Capacity

Vocabulary

Complete.

1. _____ is the amount a container can hold
   when filled.

2. Use the words *cup*, *pint*, *quart*, *gallon* to label the capacity.

_____   _____   _____   _____

Circle the letter of the reasonable unit.

3. **a.** pt   **b.** gal   4. **a.** pt   **b.** gal   5. **a.** c   **b.** gal

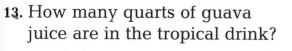  

Write the equivalent measurement.

6. 12 pt = _____ c   7. 4 c = _____ qt   8. 3 qt = _____ c

9. 16 qt = _____ gal   10. 2 gal = _____ pt   11. 1 gal = _____ c

Mixed Applications

For Problems 12–13, use the recipe.

12. How many cups does the recipe make?

_____

13. How many quarts of guava juice are in the tropical drink?

_____

Tropical Drink
1 qt pineapple juice
1 gal guava juice
1 qt mango juice

Name _____

Weight

Vocabulary

Complete.

1. A bread truck weighs about 1 _____.

2. A slice of bread weighs about 1 _____.

3. A loaf of bread weighs about 1 _____.

Choose the more reasonable measurement.

4. 1,200 lb or 1,200 oz

_____

5. 10 T or 10 lb

_____

6. 168 oz or 168 lb

_____

7. 1 lb or 1 oz

_____

8. 15 T or 15 lb

_____

9. 12 oz or 12 lb

_____

Write the equivalent measurement. You may use a calculator.

10. 2 lb = _____ oz

11. 4 T = _____ lb

12. 60,000 lb = _____ T

13. 64 oz = _____ lb

14. 1 T = _____ oz

15. 208 oz = _____ lb

Mixed Applications

For Problem 16, use the picture.

16. How many baby elephants equal the weight of the adult elephant?

_____

Linear Measures

Vocabulary

Complete.

1. A(n) _____ is about the width of your index finger.

2. A(n) _____ is equal to 10 centimeters and is about the width of an adult's hand.

3. A(n) _____ is about the distance from one hand to the other when you stretch out your arms.

Use a centimeter ruler or a meterstick to measure each thing. Write the measurement and unit of measure you used.

4. length of your desk   5. width of a piece of chalk   6. height of a door

_____   _____   _____

Choose the most reasonable measurement. Write a, b, or c.

7. _____   width of a head   **a.** 2 cm   **b.** 2 dm   **c.** 2 m

8. _____   distance around   **a.** 1,000 cm   **b.** 1,000 dm   **c.** 1,000 m
             the school

9. _____   height of a tree   **a.** 5 cm   **b.** 5 dm   **c.** 5 m

10. _____   width across   **a.** 22 cm   **b.** 22 dm   **c.** 22 m
             notebook paper

Mixed Applications

11. Bill has a piece of tape that is 24 cm long. Phil has a piece of tape 3 dm long. Who has the longer piece of tape? How much longer?

12. Lonnie bought a pencil that was 12 cm long. Pat bought one at the circus that was 5 times as long. How long is Pat's pencil?

_____   _____

Name _____

LESSON
25.2

Decimals and Metric Measures

Write the missing unit. Use a meterstick to help you.

1. 3 _____ = 300 cm

2. 7 _____ = 70 cm

3. 0.08 _____ = 8 cm

4. 14 _____ = 140 dm

5. 0.25 _____ = 2.5 dm

6. 0.1 _____ = 1 cm

7. 12 _____ = 120 cm

8. 0.05 _____ = 5 cm

Write the decimal number. Use a meterstick to help you.

9. 3 cm = _____ m

10. 8 dm = _____ m

11. 9 cm = _____ m

12. 12 dm = _____ m

13. 24 dm = _____ m

14. 90 cm = _____ m

15. 2 dm = _____ m

16. 70 cm = _____ m

Mixed Applications

17. Hope's arm is 4.5 dm in length. Is her arm longer or shorter than 5 cm? What is her arm length in meters?

18. Write a problem about measuring an item in your school. Then write that measurement in centimeters, decimeters, or meters.

_____

_____

_____

19. Todd is making a border around a picture. He has two pieces of border. They measure 120 cm and 95 cm. Does he have enough border for the picture? Explain.

42 cm

57 cm   57 cm

42 cm

20. Tim and Rich are making tails for their kites. Tim's kite tail is 0.8 m longer than Rich's kite tail. Rich's kite tail is 1.2 m long. How many meters long is Tim's kite tail?

P152   ON MY OWN

Changing Units

Would you multiply each by 10 or by 100 to change the larger
units to the smaller units? Write × *10* or × *100*.

1. 6 m = ? cm _____

2. 12 dm = ? cm _____

3. 6 dm = ? cm _____

4. 2 dm = ? cm _____

5. 4 m = ? dm _____

6. 5 m = ? cm _____

Fill in the missing measures. You may use a calculator.

	Meters	Decimeters	Centimeters
7.	2		200
8.		110	1,100
9.	17	170	
10.		70	700
11.	3	30	
12.	26		2,600

Write the equivalent measurement. You may use a calculator.

13. 8 dm = _____ cm

14. 32 m = _____ cm

15. 3 dm = _____ cm

16. 16 m = _____ dm

17. 19 m = _____ dm

18. 48 m = _____ cm

Mixed Applications

For Problems 19–20, use the floor plan and measurements of Tally's clubhouse.

19. What is the perimeter in meters
of Tally's clubhouse?

_____

20. How many centimeters are
between the toy box and the
counter?

_____

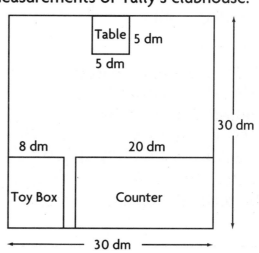

Name _____

Problem-Solving Strategy

Solve a Simpler Problem

Solve a simpler problem.

1. Sarah grew a zucchini that is 3.5 decimeters long. How many centimeters long is her zucchini?

2. Thomas has saved $3.80 in dimes. How many dimes has he saved?

3. Sophia's dog is 44 centimeters tall. Claudia's dog is 7 decimeters tall. Who has the taller dog? How many centimeters taller is the dog?

4. A rectangular area that is 5 feet by 7 feet is being enclosed with posts and fencing. A post will be used every 6 inches. How many posts will be used?

Mixed Applications

Solve.

CHOOSE A STRATEGY

• Make an Organized List • Work Backward • Write a Number Sentence • Guess and Check

5. There are 30 people attending the dinner. Each table will hold the same number of people, except for the speaker's table. The speaker's table will have 6 people. There are more than 4 tables. How many tables are needed in all?

6. Tamara has 38 stickers she wants to give to 7 friends. She wants them all to have the same amount. How many stickers does each friend get? How many stickers are left over?

7. The O'Henrys' rented 2 surfboards, 3 boogie boards, and 1 skateboard for 5 hours. How much did they spend?

BEACH RENTALS	
Surfboards	$12/day
Boogie Boards	$8/day
Skateboards	$2/hour

Capacity

Vocabulary

Complete.

1. A _____ is about the size of a sports-drink bottle. It contains 1,000 milliliters.

2. A _____ is about the size of a drop of liquid in an eyedropper.

Choose the reasonable unit of measure. Write *mL, metric cup,* or *L.*

3. wading pool   4. a soda can   5. a baby bottle

_____   _____   _____

Choose the most reasonable measurement. Write *a, b,* or *c.*

6. _____   **a.** 3 mL   **b.** 30 mL   **c.** 3 L

7. _____   **a.** 42 mL   **b.** 420 mL   **c.** 42 L

8. _____   **a.** 62 mL   **b.** 620 mL   **c.** 62 L

9. _____   **a.** 150 mL   **b.** 1,500 mL   **c.** 150 L

10. _____   **a.** 8 mL   **b.** 80 mL   **c.** 8 L

Mixed Applications

11. It is good to drink at least 8 glasses of water a day. If a glass holds about 250 mL, how many liters is that?

_____

12. In Germany gas sells for $1.15 per liter (in United States dollars). How much would it cost for 2 liters of gasoline?

_____

Name _____

Mass

Vocabulary

Write the letter of the word that is best described.

1. _____ the amount of mass that is about equal to a baseball bat

2. _____ the amount of matter in an object

3. _____ the amount of mass that is about equal to a large paper clip

a. kilogram (kg)

b. gram (g)

c. mass

Choose the more reasonable measurement. Write *g* or *kg*.

4.   5.   6.   7.   8.

_____   _____   _____   _____   _____

Choose the more reasonable measurement.

9.   10.   11.   12.

1 g or 1 kg   5 g or 5 kg   200 g or 20 kg   600 g or 600 kg

_____   _____   _____   _____

Mixed Applications

13. A box of macaroni and cheese makes 3 servings. Each serving is 70 g. How many grams of food does the box make?

_____

14. John bought 2 boxes of macaroni and cheese for $0.98 each. What was the cost for both boxes?

_____

Time as a Fraction

Write each time in a different way.

1. 2:30   **2.** 8:45   **3.** 6:15

_____   _____   _____

4. 4:45   **5.** a quarter past one   **6.** half past five

_____   _____   _____

7. a quarter to eleven   **8.** half past six   **9.** a quarter past seven

_____   _____   _____

Use *a quarter* or *half* to express the time shown.

10.

11.

12.

_____   _____   _____

13.

14.

15.

_____   _____   _____

Mixed Applications

16. A movie started at 1:45 and ended 90 minutes later. How can you use *a quarter* or *half* to express the time that the movie ended?

_____

17. Melissa bought 3 pounds of apples that cost $1.49 per pound. What is the total amount of Melissa's purchase?

_____

Choosing Customary or Metric Units

Find the perimeter of each figure in customary and metric units.

1.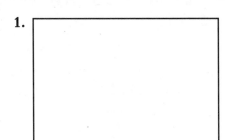

_____

2.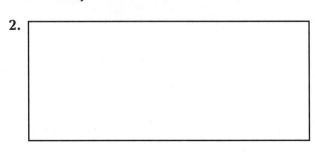

_____

3.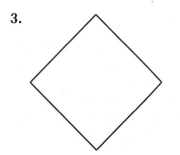

_____

4.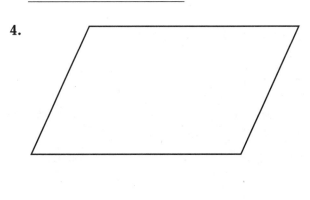

_____

Choose the most reasonable measure for what is shown.

5. ├———————┤

2.5 in. or 2.5 cm?

_____

6. ├————————————————┤

3 in. or 3 cm?

_____

Mixed Applications

7. Carolyn's teacher asks her to get 3 x 5 cards from the supply cabinet. Does the teacher mean 3 in. × 5 in. or 3 cm × 5 cm?

_____

8. The 24 students in Ms. Spedden's class raised $384 for a local charity. Each student raised the same amount of money. How much did each student raise?

_____

Problem-Solving Strategy

Write a Number Sentence

Write a number sentence to solve.

1. Jorge's parents are painting a border around their chicken coop. The coop is 18 feet long and 15 feet wide. What is the perimeter of the border in yards?

_____

_____

2. Joel buys four items costing $38, $47, $78, and $25. He receives a $39 discount. What is the total price that Joel will pay?

_____

_____

3. Mihn buys 4 ribbons to complete a costume for the school play. The lengths of the ribbons are 25 cm, 40 cm, 55 cm, and 80 cm. How many meters of ribbon does she need?

_____

_____

4. Hovik goes to the movies with his two parents and two sisters. Tickets are $7.50 for adults and $3.75 for children. What is the total cost for tickets for Hovik's family?

_____

_____

Mixed Applications

Solve.

CHOOSE A STRATEGY

• **Work Backward** • **Make an Organized List** • **Make a Graph** • **Act It Out** • **Draw a Diagram**

5. Peggy spent $5 at lunch. Then she spent half her money at the school fair. She bought a present with half her remaining money. Peggy has $9 left. How much money did Peggy begin with?

_____

6. Ben made 2 pans of brownies. He cut each pan into 12 bars. When two friends arrive, Ben divides the brownies equally among everyone. How many brownies will each person receive?

_____

Temperature

Vocabulary

Fill in the blank.

1. _____ are customary units for measuring temperature.

2. _____ are metric units for measuring temperature.

Use the thermometer to answer the question.

3. 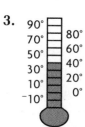 The outdoor temperature is shown. The indoor temperature is 72°F. What is the difference between the two temperatures?

_____

4. 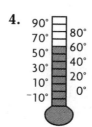 The ocean water temperature is shown. The air temperature is 94°F. What is the difference between the two temperatures?

_____

Write the difference between the two temperatures.

5. 32°F and 71°F _____

6. 67°C and ⁻15°C _____

7. 67°F and 29°F _____

8. 48°C and ⁻10°C _____

Mixed Applications

9. At noon it was 31°C. By sundown, it had cooled down 8 degrees. At dawn, it was 11 degrees cooler. What was the temperature at dawn?

_____

10. Meg ran 1 mile in 5 minutes, 36 seconds. Ellen ran 1 mile in 5 minutes, 52 seconds. Who ran faster? Explain.

_____

_____

Making Equal Areas

Trace and cut out the pattern-block shapes. Use them to model each area.

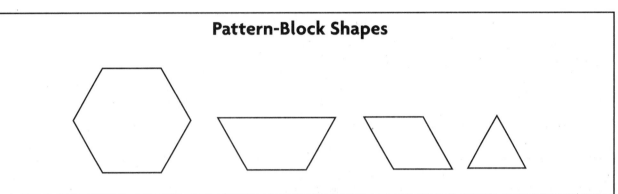

Pattern-Block Shapes

1. Use ⬡ as the whole. Model $\frac{1}{2}$.

2. Use ▱ as the whole. Model $\frac{1}{2}$.

3. Use △ as the whole. Model $\frac{1}{3}$.

4. Use ⬡ as the whole. Model $\frac{1}{3}$.

5. Use △ as the whole. Model $\frac{2}{3}$.

6. Use ⬡ as the whole. Model $\frac{2}{3}$.

Mixed Applications

7. Trevor is making a tile design. He has some ▲ and some ▼. How can Trevor use some of each shape to make a hexagon?

_____

_____

8. Cassette tapes come in packages of 12 or 16. Jenny orders 5 packages and gets a total of 76 tapes. How many 12-packs and how many 16-packs did Jenny order?

_____

9. Paula, Ming-Lei, and Maria shared the money they earned at a garage sale. There were 5 one-dollar bills, 3 quarters, 2 dimes, and 5 pennies. How much money did each girl receive?

_____

10. Pierre has 9 blank pages in his yearbook. He wants 126 fourth-grade students to sign his book. He wants an equal number of signatures on each blank page. How many will sign each page?

_____

Division Patterns to Estimate

Write the numbers you would use to estimate the quotient.
Then write the estimate.

1. $58 \div 15 = n$ **2.** $695 \div 65 = n$ **3.** $556 \div 68 = n$

_____   _____   _____

4. $273 \div 32 = n$ **5.** $447 \div 52 = n$ **6.** $810 \div 42 = n$

_____   _____   _____

Write the basic fact that helps you find the quotient.

7. $45 \div 14 = n$ **8.** $362 \div 64 = n$ **9.** $596 \div 34 = n$

_____   _____   _____

10. $64 \div 19 = n$ **11.** $238 \div 83 = n$ **12.** $721 \div 78 = n$

_____   _____   _____

Complete the table.

	Dividend	Divisor	Quotient
13.	60	$\div 30$	_____
14.	_____	$\div 30$	20
15.	6,000	$\div 30$	_____
16.	_____	$\div 30$	2,000

Mixed Applications

17. The Stones had 87 people at the family reunion. They played softball with 9 people on each team. About how many teams played softball?

_____

18. In class there are 31 students. Mr. Oliver bought 242 pencils for the class. About how many pencils will each student get?

_____

Dividing by Tens

Draw a box where the first digit in the quotient should be placed.

1. $30\overline{)82}$ 2. $20\overline{)822}$ 3. $70\overline{)940}$ 4. $50\overline{)218}$

5. $40\overline{)520}$ 6. $60\overline{)380}$ 7. $80\overline{)571}$ 8. $90\overline{)684}$

Find the quotient.

9. $20\overline{)435}$ 10. $60\overline{)824}$ 11. $40\overline{)372}$ 12. $70\overline{)285}$

13. $50\overline{)675}$ 14. $30\overline{)729}$ 15. $90\overline{)458}$ 16. $80\overline{)726}$

Mixed Applications

17. You have 480 index cards to divide among 12 classmates. The teacher would like 24 of the cards for a game. How many index cards does each classmate get?

18. In school today there are 15 more girls than boys. There are 250 boys. How many students are at school?

_____

Modeling Division

Make a model and find the quotient.

1. $15\overline{)67}$　　　　2. $28\overline{)118}$　　　　3. $21\overline{)85}$

4. $32\overline{)100}$　　　　5. $35\overline{)176}$　　　　6. $37\overline{)115}$

7. $78 \div 25 =$ _____　　8. $97 \div 13 =$ _____　　9. $117 \div 22 =$ _____

Use the model to complete the number sentence.

10. 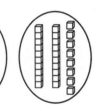　　　　$61 \div 28 =$ _____

11. 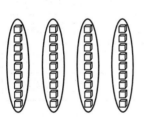　　　　$38 \div 9 =$ _____

Mixed Applications

12. Tommy wants to save $160 to go on vacation. He can save $19 a week. How many weeks will it take Tommy to save enough money?

13. The Smith children earned $145. The money will be divided evenly among the 4 children. How much money will each child get? How much money is left over?

_____　　_____

Division Procedures

Write the missing numbers for each problem.

1.
```
      1█ r1
  14)197
  -█4
    5█
  -56
    1
```

2.
```
      23 r█
  28)647
  -5█
    8█
  -84
    3
```

3.
```
      █7 r8
  32)872
  -64
    23█
  -22█
    8
```

Find the quotient. Check by multiplying.

4. 17)206

5. 19)81

6. 23)485

7. 28)150

Mixed Applications

For Problems 8–10, use the table.

8. Stanley's family drove from Los Angeles to San Francisco. They drove about 60 miles per hour. How many hours did it take Stanley's family to complete the trip?

_____

_____

MILES FROM LOS ANGELES	
City	Distance
San Diego	120 miles
San Francisco	377 miles
Phoenix	425 miles
Seattle	1,302 miles

9. The Wilson family spent 15 hours bicycling from Los Angeles to San Diego. They traveled the same number of miles each hour. How many miles did they bicycle each hour?

_____

10. Write a problem that can be solved by dividing. Use the information in the table.

_____

_____

_____

Problem-Solving Strategy

Write a Number Sentence

Write a number sentence to solve.

1. Sally threw the softball 250 inches, and Mary threw the softball 20 feet. What is the distance in feet that Sally threw the softball? Who threw the softball farther?

_____

_____

2. Ted's little brother is 32 months old today. Rachel's little brother is 3 years old today. How many years old is Ted's little brother? Who is older?

_____

_____

3. Sam finished his chores in 15 minutes. Rafael did his chores in 850 seconds. How many minutes did it take Rafael to do his chores? Who did his chores faster?

_____

_____

4. The Fun Times Arcade has a skiing game that lasts 11 minutes. The arcade is open 14 hours a day. How many times can the skiing game be played in one day? How many extra minutes are there?

_____

_____

Mixed Applications

Solve.

CHOOSE A STRATEGY

• **Make a Model**   • **Guess and Check**   • **Work Backward**   • **Write a Number Sentence**

5. Tobias needs the following to make a poster: $\frac{1}{3}$ sheet of blue poster board, $\frac{1}{6}$ sheet of yellow poster board, and $\frac{1}{4}$ sheet of green poster board. Order these fractions from the least to the greatest.

_____

6. Anthony had $2.25 when he got home from the arcade. He spent $4.50 on video games, $3.75 on miniature golf, and $1.25 on snacks. Then Henry gave Anthony $1.50. How much money did Anthony have when he left home?

_____

Correcting Quotients

Write *too high, too low,* or *just right* for each estimate. Find the quotient.

1. $17\overline{)152}$ 8   _____

     _____

2. $35\overline{)186}$ 4   _____

     _____

3. $42\overline{)351}$ 7   _____

     _____

4. $48\overline{)374}$ 8   _____

     _____

5. $52\overline{)419}$ 7   _____

     _____

6. $76\overline{)679}$ 8   _____

     _____

7. $63\overline{)556}$ 9   _____

     _____

8. $67\overline{)650}$ 9   _____

     _____

Mixed Applications

9. Sue is packing 116 spools of thread into shoe boxes. Each box can hold 42 spools of thread. Will Sue be able to pack all the spools into 2 boxes? Explain.

_____

_____

10. Tony is estimating the time he needs to complete his math homework. He can complete about 3 problems per minute. If he allows 20 minutes, will he finish his 42 math problems? Explain.

_____

_____

Making a Circle Graph

Vocabulary

1. A graph that is in the shape of a circle and shows data as a

   whole made up of different parts is a _____ .

Label each graph.

2. a group of puppies, $\frac{1}{2}$ of which are brown, $\frac{1}{4}$ black, and $\frac{1}{4}$ spotted

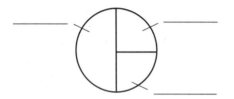

3. a petting zoo that is $\frac{1}{2}$ goats, $\frac{3}{8}$ sheep, and $\frac{1}{8}$ rabbits

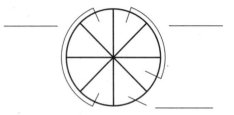

4. a fruit salad that is $\frac{1}{2}$ bananas, $\frac{1}{6}$ strawberries, $\frac{1}{6}$ blueberries, and $\frac{1}{6}$ peaches

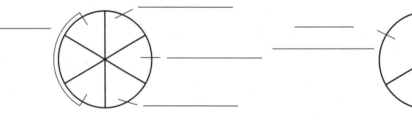

5. a CD collection that is $\frac{2}{3}$ rock and roll and $\frac{1}{3}$ movie soundtracks

Mixed Applications

6. There were 920 people at the first baseball game and 1,010 people at the second game. How many more people were at the second game?

   _____

7. Jamie baked 5 dozen cookies on Monday. By Friday, only 7 cookies were left. How many cookies were eaten?

   _____

Fractions in Circle Graphs

For Problems 1–7, use the circle graphs.

1. What fraction of the 28 students walk to school? ride the bus?

   _____

2. Is the fraction of students who are driven by a parent greater than or less than the fraction of students who ride the bus?

   _____

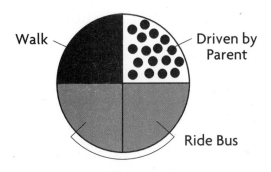

Transportation
of 28 Students to School

3. What fraction represents all the students in the transportation survey?

   _____

4. What fraction of the 6 students own hamsters? cats?

   _____

5. The fraction $\frac{1}{6}$ represents the students who own which animals?

   _____

   _____

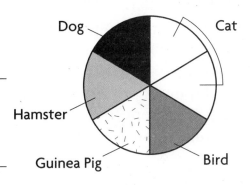

Pets Owned
by 6 Students

6. What fraction represents all the students in the pet survey?

   _____

Mixed Applications

7. Look at the circle graph for *Pets Owned.* If, starting on a Tuesday, 1 pet is taken to a veterinarian each school day, on what day would the last pet be taken?

   _____

8. Mr. Kaimal paid for 6 concert tickets with three $20 bills. He received $7.50 in change. What was the price of 1 concert ticket?

   _____

Decimals in Circle Graphs

For Problems 1–3, use the circle graph.

1. What does the whole circle graph show?

   _____

   _____

2. What decimal tells how many of the classes danced in the show?

   _____

3. What decimal tells how many of the classes presented a skit in the performance?

   _____

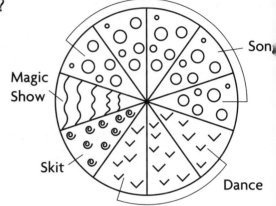

Magic
Show

Skit

Son,

Dance

**Performances Given
by 10 Classes in Variety Show**

4. Complete the circle graph to show the following data:

   Marisa has a collection of 10 stamps. Of the stamps, 3 are from Mexico, 3 are from Japan, 2 are from Africa, 1 is from India, and 1 is from Ireland.

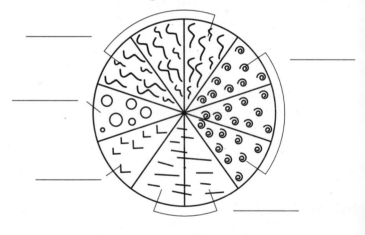

Mixed Applications

5. Adam has a collection of 60 coins. Of the coins, 10 are from the United States, 10 are from Canada, 20 are from Mexico, 10 are from Central America, and the rest are from Asia. How many coins are from Asia?

   _____

6. Use the circle divided into 6 equal parts. Show the data about coin collection listed in Exercise 5.

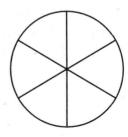

Problem-Solving Strategy

Make a Graph

Make a graph and solve.

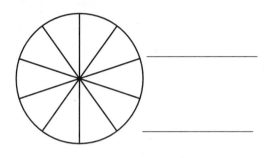 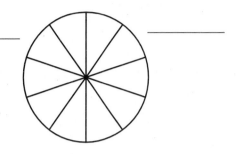

1. The members of the Dog-Walkers Club are having a pizza party. They are deciding what toppings to get. Of the 10 members, 7 want mushrooms, 2 want pepperoni, and 1 wants anchovies. What decimal tells how many want mushrooms? pepperoni? anchovies?

   _____

2. Meg asked 10 students if they preferred swimming in a pool, a lake, or an ocean. Of the students Meg asked, 6 said pool, 1 said lake, and 3 said ocean. What decimal tells how many prefer a pool?

   _____

Mixed Applications

Solve.

CHOOSE A STRATEGY

- **Find a Pattern**   - **Act It Out**   - **Draw a Diagram**   - **Write a Number Sentence**

3. A series of numbers starts with $\frac{1}{4}$. Each number in the series is two times greater than the number before it. What is the sixth number in the series?

4. Jim folded a strip of paper in half, and then in half again, and then in half once more. When he opened up the folded strip of paper, how many sections did he see?

Choosing Graphs to Represent Data

Match the graph with the set of data it describes.

a.

Bagels — Muffins

Donuts

1. $\frac{2}{4}$ bagels

   $\frac{1}{4}$ donuts

   $\frac{1}{4}$ muffins

   _____

b.

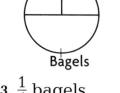

Bagels — Donuts

Muffins — Danish

2. $\frac{1}{4}$ bagels

   $\frac{1}{4}$ donuts

   $\frac{2}{4}$ muffins

   _____

c.

Muffins — Donuts

Bagels

3. $\frac{1}{4}$ bagels

   $\frac{2}{4}$ donuts

   $\frac{1}{4}$ muffins

   _____

d.

Bagels — Donuts

Muffins

4. $\frac{1}{4}$ bagels

   $\frac{1}{4}$ donuts

   $\frac{1}{4}$ muffins

   $\frac{1}{4}$ Danish

   _____

Mixed Applications

For Problems 5 and 6, use the *Sea Creature* circle graph.

5. What does the whole circle represent?

   _____

   _____

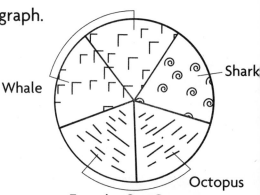

Whale

Shark

Octopus

**Favorite Sea Creature
Choices of 25 Students**

6. Write a fraction to represent each part of the graph.

   _____

7. Don makes a pie filling that is $\frac{1}{2}$ strawberries, $\frac{1}{4}$ blueberries, and $\frac{1}{4}$ cranberries. What decimal represents the amount of strawberries? blueberries? cranberries? Complete the circle graph to solve.

   _____

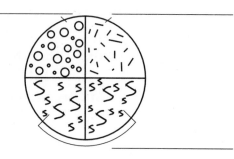